sunny days & easy living

RYLAND
PETERS
& SMALL
LONDON NEW YORK

sunny days & easy living

relaxed food to enjoy outdoors

Lindy Wildsmith
photography by Martin Brigdale

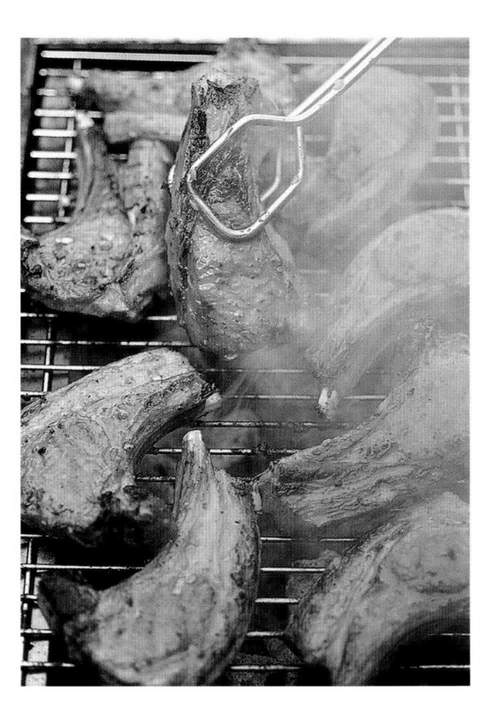

Dedication

For all my family and friends who make eating outdoors such fun.

Design and Art Direction Steve Painter
Commissioning Editor Elsa Petersen-Schepelern
Editors Rachel Lawrence, Susan Stuck
Production Paul Harding
Art Director Anne-Marie Bulat
Publishing Director Alison Starling

Food Stylist Bridget Sargeson
Prop Stylist Helen Trent
Indexer Hilary Bird

Notes

• All spoon measurements are level, unless otherwise stated.

• Eggs are medium, unless otherwise specified. Uncooked or partially cooked eggs should not be served to the very old, frail, young children, pregnant women, or those with compromised immune systems.

• Ovens should be preheated to the specified temperature. Recipes in this book were tested using a regular oven. If using a fan-assisted oven, follow the manufacturer's instructions for adjusting temperatures.

Originally published in hardcover as *Eating Outdoors* in the United States in 2006.

This paperback edition published in 2010
by Ryland Peters & Small, Inc.
619 Broadway, 6th Floor
New York, NY 10012
www.rylandpeters.com

10 9 8 7 6 5 4 3 2 1

ISBN: 978 1 84597 988 1

The hardcover edition is cataloged as follows:
Library of Congress Cataloging-in-Publication Data

Wildsmith, Lindy.
Eating outdoors : cooking and entertaining in the open air / Lindy Wildsmith ; photography by Martin Brigdale.
p. cm.
Includes bibliographical references and index.
1. Outdoor cookery. 2. Entertaining. I. Title.
TX823.W513 2006
641.5'78--dc22

2005033082

Printed and bound in China.

contents

food tastes better outdoors

Once spring is in the air and we can feel the warmth of the sun, our thoughts drift back to the wonderful meals we have shared with family and friends in summers past. Enjoy a family meal in the early summer sun, cook a barbecue in the comforting shade of home, mix drinks at sunset, dine under the stars, or picnic in the great outdoors and the memory will linger. Eating outdoors is about making the most of what nature has to offer and turning something ordinary into something extraordinary. Whether it is a simple snack or an elegant meal, food always tastes better outside. Make a Florida Refresher (page 132) and a stack of Scotch Pancakes (page 67) for breakfast and eat at leisure in the open air. The freshness of the morning and the sun on your face will instantly put you in a holiday mood.

Come the summer, the pull of the outdoors is irresistible. We all have a favorite picnic tryst, be it in a nearby park or garden, or far away in the countryside. Rather than making a mountain of rolls or sandwiches, try a Sicilian hooded sandwich, or *cabbucio*, filled with cheese, tomato, and salami (page 78). Wrap it in foil and a cloth and off you go! Cooking outside is the ultimate in summer entertainment and a cook-out, whether it be in your own back yard or at a suitable local beauty spot, is fun for everyone. There are recipes for every taste, including Vegetable Kabobs with Bagna Cauda Dressing (page 40), Foil-wrapped Trout with Prosciutto, Olives, and Mushrooms (page 39) and Aromatic Pork Burger in Pita Bread with Chile Tomato Chutney (page 24).

Everyone loves their outside space. There may only be room for a tiny table, a couple of chairs, and a flower pot or two, but it will be a special place where you can get away from it all. Plan a simple but elegant menu and luxuriate in the occasion. Outdoor food need not necessarily involve extra work, but it does help to plan ahead and to be organized so you can enjoy the occasion, too. The book therefore opens with practical hints and suggestions covering Grilling Know-how (page 9), Perfect Picnics (page 10) and Al Fresco Dining (page 11).

Sunny Days & Easy Living is packed full of original and traditional recipes to inspire you into the kitchen and out into the fresh air. There are clear, concise instructions and many of the dishes can be prepared in advance. Small or large scale, a sandwich or a spread, there is nothing as pleasing as eating outdoors.

grilling know-how

Getting the grill out is a sure sign of summer. Time to crack open a few beers, pull a cork or two, and invite friends round. It does not have to be an elaborate affair—in fact, the simpler, the better. The smell of food cooking in the open air stimulates everyone's appetite and it is the kind of occasion when you can ask your guests to bring food and start the cooking when they arrive.

One of the dangers of a cook-out is finishing up with a mountain of charred meat all tasting the same. To avoid this, I have included recipes for colorful relishes and salsas, such as Mango, Kiwi, and Cilantro Salsa (page 15), delicious salads like Fennel and Orange Salad with Mint and Olives (page 16), and unusual grilled vegetable recipes, like Sesame Sweet Potato Packages (page 20). There are mouthwatering recipes for seafood, meat, and poultry—everything from Spiked Tiger Shrimp with Lime and Chile Marinade (page 36) to Nick's Barbecued Rare Roast Beef (page 31). For those who prefer to stay in the kitchen, the recipes contain instructions on cooking them indoors. The results are just as good and there is no fear of burning the food if your attention wanders to the guests and your glass of wine. For an extra flourish, the food can be put on the grill for a few minutes just before serving.

Choosing an outdoor grill

Most grills are charcoal or wood burners, although gas and electric ones are becoming increasingly popular. Traditional charcoal grills need time and patience to get going, whereas a gas grill is more or less instant. It does not give that traditional barbecue flavor, however, and requires a heavy gas cylinder.

You will also a few pieces of equipment, including long-handled utensils, such as tongs and metal spatulas, as well as tongs for the coals, a rake for the embers and a stiff wire brush for cleaning the grill rack. A small sharp knife is essential for cutting into meat and fish to see if it is thoroughly cooked. You may also need thick oven mitts. A pre-heated ridged grill pan set over the grill rack is ideal for cooking steaks, fish and vegetables as it seals the flavor inside and leaves attractive char-grilled stripes on the outside.

Lighting a charcoal grill

Choose a sheltered spot out of the wind and try to site the grill where the smoke will not waft over your guests or into the neighboring property. Be considerate, not everyone loves the smell of the grill! Make sure you light the grill an hour before you want to eat to ensure you are cooking on embers not flames. So often the grill is at its best when there is no more food to cook. Break a few firelighters in half and mix them with a few pieces of charcoal, then put them in the middle of the grill. Pile on more charcoal to a depth of 2–4 inches and light. When the coals start to glow, spread them out to cover the base. When the flames have died down and there is no smoke, and the coals are glowing and covered with a powdery grey surface they are ready. This whole process will take 45–60 minutes.

Cooking on the grill

Once the coals are ready, arrange the meat on the grill and give it time to brown before turning. Once the meat has browned, turn it frequently and move it around the grill to ensure even cooking. You may need to raise the grill height if the cooking is too fast, or lower it so that it is nearer the coals if it is too slow. To lower the heat, dampen the coals slightly or close the air vent.

When using frozen meat or fish, ensure it is properly thawed before you start cooking. Make sure you cook chicken, burgers, and sausages thoroughly. They should be piping hot all the way through, none of the meat should be pink, and the juices should run clear. Cut into meats such as chicken to make sure they are cooked thoroughly. Cross contamination is one of the major causes of food poisoning, so it is essential to keep raw and cooked food apart.

Preparing the food

Get all the preparation done in advance—the day, the morning or an hour or two before you eat. Marinating times in the recipes are flexible, given as 1–24 hours so do what suits you. Salsas, relishes, dressings, and salads can be made in advance, but green salads should be dressed at the last minute. Cover the food once prepared and refrigerate or store it in a cool place until you are ready to cook or serve it.

Safety tips

- Site the barbecue on level ground away from sheds, fences, and trees.
- Consider wind direction before lighting as sparks can cause fires.
- Use charcoal, briquettes or firelighters; don't use gasoline or paraffin to get the grill started.
- Keep a bucket of water or sand, or a garden hose nearby.
- Keep children, pets, and garden games away from the grill.
- Leave the embers to cool completely before disposing of them.

perfect picnics

Picnics are a bit like Christmas, once you have organized everything you can switch off, relax, and enjoy yourself and this is one of the reasons I love them. My picnics fall into two categories. The first is a simple spread, like those I remember from my childhood, of fresh seasonal produce, packed into boxes and bags. Everyone sits on a blanket on the ground and helps themselves, there are no plates, no cutlery, and no fuss. Such a picnic is the ideal solution to a day on the beach or a foray into the countryside. Alternatively, they are grand occasions with shades of the British Raj, using tables, chairs, serving dishes, glasses, candles and flowers. These sort of picnics are perfect for a family get-together, a celebration, a special sporting event, or an outdoor concert.

Putting a picnic together

Although it is fun to plan and organize a picnic, it can often be a spur of the moment thing and you don't always want to go to the trouble of making a lot of fancy food. A last minute trip to your local delicatessen to buy cold meats, canned or smoked fish, eggs, sausages, pies, pâtés, and cheeses will solve the problem. Add fresh strawberries, cherries, tomatoes and cold drinks, and you have all you need. With a little extra time you can rustle up a filled loaf (pages 78–83) and make some dips (page 85) to serve with vegetables sticks. Try a single dish salad, such as Cherry Tomato Tabbouleh Salad with Pastrami (page 90), and bake a sweet treat (pages 93–97). For the really big occasion, try my Layered Salmon, Shrimp, and Potato Filo Pie (page 77) flavored with tomato and basil. It will make a wonderful centerpiece and yet is easy to make.

Lastly, don't limit yourself to the picnic section of the book as there are delicious ideas and recipes for feasting outdoors throughout the book.

Children's picnics

Small children love to picnic on simple fare. Put raw vegetable sticks, cherry tomatoes, chicken legs, fruit, and Triple Chocolate Chip Muffins (page 94) in a basket and send them out to the garden and see what fun they have. Pack up their backpacks with jelly sandwiches or some freshly made scones (page 70) and take them on a walk or bike ride in the countryside and they will think they are in heaven. These are moments—believe it or not—they will remember to adulthood.

Packing your picnic

Transfer chilled food from the fridge to your coolers just before you leave. Pack as much food as possible in plastic boxes to prevent it getting squashed. Put the boxes in first, followed by the frozen ice packs. Put anything that might get squashed on top. Pack warm food separately in a basket. Pack chilled drinks in a separate cooler and if your picnic extends into the evening take a flask of coffee or tea and a little whisky or brandy to keep you warm.

Keeping food cold

When the weather is hot, it is essential to keep food and drink cool and to take plenty of water. Picnic hampers are beautiful, but do not keep food cold so use them to transport plates, cutlery, glasses, and flasks and extras such as bread, nibbles and fruit that do not need to be chilled. Rather than buying a very large coolers, two smaller ones are often more practical. Freeze a couple of large bottles of water and pack them in the bottom of your bags to keep the picnic cold and provide extra cool water for later. At your destination, store the picnic in a cool, shady spot and keep the bags closed when not in use. On the beach, you can throw a wet towel over the coolers to keep them cold.

Picnic essentials

- One large or two smaller coolers with ice packs.
- Food, drink, and water.
- Blanket/groundcloth or chairs and table.
- Basket to carry plates, cutlery, and glasses.
- Bottle opener and corkscrew.
- Flasks of boiling water, plus what you need to make tea and coffee.
- Large trash bag to take trash home.

al fresco dining

We all long to recreate the wonder of eating outdoors on holiday, whether it be a long lunch in cool, leafy shade on a stifling hot day, a candlelit dinner in the balmy evening air, or a night spent chatting into the early hours. The weather may not always be as reliable at home, but when we are able to dine *al fresco*, it is a truly magical occasion.

Getting organized

As with all entertaining, it helps to be organized. When choosing a menu, think about what is in season and don't to be too rigid when shopping. If you are inviting new friends find out if they are vegetarian or have any food intolerances to ingredients such as wheat, seafood, nuts, or dairy products. A vegetarian menu of Chilled Spinach, Arugula, and Watercress Soup (page 103), Risotto with Sicilian Pesto (page 118) and Blueberry Frangipane Tart (page 126) would be eminently suitable and popular with non-vegetarians too. When choosing a menu for a special diet, cook it for everyone, otherwise you will just be making extra work for yourself. Once you have decided what you are going to cook, work out how much food you need—it's always better to make too much food so you don't run short. Make a shopping list and don't forget extras such as bread, chocolates, flowers, candles, nibbles, drinks and extra ice. You don't want to have to go back to the store at the last minute.

Give yourself plenty of time to prepare and cook the food and don't choose complicated recipes you have not made before. Go for recipes that can be prepared or cooked in advance and baked or reheated when your guests arrive. It is your party and you should enjoy it too. Alternatively, if your *al fresco* meal is an impromptu tête-à-tête or a family treat at the end of a busy day you may prefer a last minute menu, such as Speck and Crayfish Cichetti Laced with Chile (page 104), Instant Seafood Spaghetti (page 111), and Pineapple, Mango, Avocado, and Banana with White Rum and Mint (page 125).

Drinks should be kept chilled until the last minute. If you are short of refrigerator space, put bottles and cans in a large receptacle in a shady spot and cover them with cold water and ice. If you are making a punch, such as Trafalgar Claret Cup (page 136) or John's Jug o'Pimms (page 139), have the fruit and ice ready in the freezer. Have some interesting nonalcoholic drinks too, like Melon and Ginger Refresher (page 135).

Setting the scene

Whether you have a large garden or a small paved area you can set the scene for a leisurely lunch or an elegant candlelit dinner. You don't even need special furniture as you can simply carry a table and chairs outside or throw a rug and cushions on the ground and dine Turkish style. You actually need very little to create a successful meal outdoors; you just need to seize the moment.

Set up your table in a sheltered spot out of the wind, preferably not too far from the house, as everything will have to be carried out and in again later. At lunchtime, provide some shade—a garden parasol is the obvious solution, but the natural shade of a tree or a plant covered trellis it is far more effective and also very pretty. Set the table with everything you will need, such as plates, cutlery, napkins, glasses, and nibbles, and cover it with cloths until your guests arrive. If it is windy, make sure that any cloths are weighted down. On hot summer days we eat in the dappled shade of an old apple tree, and for birthdays we hang it with colored streamers or twinkling lanterns by night with, and in late summer it is covered with its own picture book red apples.

Dressing for dinner

Colored lights and pretty lanterns, and colorful plates, cutlery, and glasses look wonderful on an outdoor dining table. Lay the table with a cloth and all the trappings you would use indoors, including flowers and lots of candles if dining after dark. You can also fill the garden with flares and lanterns and ponds with floating candles. Finally, warn your guests that they are dining outdoors so that they come dressed appropriately and be sensible if the weather turns cold and you are forced to abandon ship and go indoors.

barbecues

Just the mention of the word barbecue is enough to excite tired winter taste buds and to inspire the chef in everyone. The barbecue is a simple escape from the confines of the kitchen and the formality of eating round the table. Whether you serve a few choice sausages with a homemade relish or an exotic menu of grilled seafood, meat, and vegetables, it's fun to cook on a fire and even more fun to eat freshly-cooked food out of doors.

mango, kiwi, and cilantro salsa

1 large ripe mango, peeled, pitted and cut into ½-inch cubes
4 kiwi fruit, peeled and cut into ½-inch cubes
finely grated zest and freshly squeezed juice of ½ unwaxed lemon
1 tablespoon extra virgin olive oil
1 tablespoon finely chopped fresh cilantro
sea salt and freshly ground black pepper

serves 4

Put the mango and kiwi fruit in a glass bowl, then add the lemon zest and juice, olive oil, and cilantro. Season with salt and pepper to taste and mix well. Cover and refrigerate until required. Serve with grilled seafood, chicken, or lamb.

peperonata

2 onions, thinly sliced
a large handful of fresh parsley, finely chopped, plus extra to serve
2 red bell peppers, deseeded and sliced
2 yellow bell peppers, deseeded and sliced
3 14-oz. cans whole plum tomatoes, drained, deseeded and chopped
sea salt and freshly ground black pepper
olive oil, for frying

serves 8

Cover the base of a heavy-based frying pan with olive oil and put over medium heat. Add the onion and parsley and fry until the onion is softened, but not browned. Add the peppers, cook until soft, then add the tomatoes. Reduce the heat, cover and cook for 1 hour, stirring from time to time. Season with salt and pepper to taste.

Serve hot or cold, sprinkled with parsley, with grilled fish, seafood, poultry, or meat.

parsley and anchovy relish

a large handful of fresh parsley
1 tablespoon salted capers, rinsed well and dried
6 anchovy fillets
grated zest of 1 unwaxed lemon
2 garlic cloves
¼ cup extra virgin olive oil

serves 4

Put the parsley, capers, anchovies, lemon zest, and garlic on a cutting board and chop together with a large kitchen knife so that all the ingredients remain identifiable but tiny. Alternatively, put the ingredients in a food processor and chop finely, but take care not to reduce them to a mush.

Transfer to a bowl and stir in the olive oil. Cover and refrigerate until required. Serve with grilled meat or fish.

chile tomato chutney

1 small piece of dried chile, to taste
2-inch piece of fresh ginger, peeled and coarsely chopped
2 garlic cloves
2 shallots
½ cup white wine vinegar
3 14-oz. cans whole plum tomatoes, drained, juice reserved, deseeded and chopped
1 cup light brown sugar

makes 2 cups

Put the chile, ginger, garlic, and shallots in a food processor and chop finely. Put the vinegar, tomatoes, and sugar into a large, heavy saucepan, add the ginger mixture and stir well.

Put the saucepan over medium heat, bring slowly to the boil, then simmer over low heat for 1½ hours or until reduced by half, stirring from time to time. Should the chutney dry out too much, add a little of the reserved tomato juice. Let cool a little, then spoon into sterilized jars and seal with a screw-top lid. Serve with grilled fish, seafood, poultry, or meat.

When it comes to al fresco meals, or any summer meal for that matter, all you really need as an accompaniment is a big bowl of fresh salad leaves with a simple dressing and plenty of good, fresh crusty bread. However, there are certain salad ingredients, such as beets, fennel, peppers, and tomatoes, that are so distinctive and delicious that they need singling out for special treatment. Here are three traditional Mediterranean recipes that do just that.

fennel and orange salad
with mint and olives

1 large fennel bulb, quartered and thinly sliced
2 large oranges, peeled, pith removed and cut into segments
a handful of fresh mint, finely chopped, plus extra sprigs to serve
2 tablespoons small red or black olives
3 tablespoons good-quality extra virgin olive oil
sea salt and freshly ground black pepper

serves 4

Put the fennel and orange in a large bowl, add the chopped mint, olives, and olive oil, then season with salt and pepper to taste. Toss the salad well, turn out onto a serving platter and top with a few sprigs of mint. Cover and leave until required.

Note Do not be tempted to add any excess orange juice when you are mixing the salad as it will make it too watery.

beet salad
with cilantro and olive oil

1 lb. small beets
3 tablespoons extra virgin olive oil
finely chopped zest of 1 unwaxed lemon
a handful of fresh cilantro or parsley, finely chopped
½ teaspoon sugar
sea salt and freshly ground black pepper

serves 4

Trim the leaves off the beets, taking care to leave the base of the stalks attached. Boil the beets in a saucepan of simmering water for 30 minutes or until tender. Drain and leave until cool enough to handle, then peel and cut into slices.

Put the sliced beets in a bowl, add the olive oil, lemon zest, cilantro, and sugar, then season with salt and pepper to taste and toss well. Cover and leave until required.

Note You may wish to wear gloves for peeling the beets to avoid staining your hands with the juices.

riviera salad

2 red bell peppers, deseeded, cut into rings and halved
3 large, firm tomatoes, thinly sliced and halved
a large handful of fresh parsley or mint, finely chopped
2 tablespoons good-quality extra virgin olive oil
sea salt and freshly ground black pepper

serves 4

Arrange alternate rows of the peppers and tomatoes on a serving plate. Sprinkle the parsley on top. Drizzle the olive oil all over the salad, and season with salt and pepper to taste. Cover and leave until required.

grilled eggplant
with tahini spread

freshly squeezed juice of 1 lemon
6 tablespoons light tahini paste
2 large eggplants, cut lengthways into 4 or 5 pieces
1 garlic clove, unpeeled and halved
1 tablespoon chopped fresh parsley
sea salt
extra virgin olive oil, for brushing and to serve

serves 4

Tahini is a tangy Middle Eastern spread made from roasted sesame seeds that is used to make dips, cakes, and confectionery. It comes in two varieties—light tahini, made with hulled seeds, and dark tahini, made with unhulled seeds. The former is rounder in flavor and more suited to the eggplant taste. Tahini can be used as a spread or dip, or with other ingredients to make a dressing.

Put the lemon juice and tahini in a bowl and mix together.

Brush the eggplant slices with olive oil, then set over a preheated hot grill, or under a preheated hot broiler, and brown on both sides.

Transfer the eggplant slices to a plate, rub with the garlic, sprinkle with salt and spread with the tahini mixture. Sprinkle with chopped parsley, drizzle with olive oil, then serve.

Variation You could use hummus, basil pesto, or olive pesto instead of the tahini paste and lemon juice.

4 red, yellow or orange bell peppers, halved lengthways and deseeded
¼ cup extra virgin olive oil
2 tablespoons balsamic vinegar
1 teaspoon coriander seeds, crushed
sea salt and freshly ground black pepper

to serve
a few sprigs of cilantro or parsley, finely chopped
2½ oz. feta cheese, crumbled (optional)

serves 4

grilled peppers
with balsamic and cilantro dressing

Peppers are one of my favorite summer vegetables. Served raw in salads or as crudités, or roasted, grilled, fried, or stewed, they add color, texture, and taste. My favorites are red ones, which are the sweetest, followed closely by the orange and yellow ones. The unripe green ones have a slightly bitter taste, but if you are a fan, use them too. Peppers grill beautifully and when peeled they have a rich velvety texture.

Put the pepper halves in a bowl, add the olive oil, vinegar, coriander seeds, salt, and pepper and mix well. Cover until required.

Put the pepper halves, cut side up, on a preheated hot grill, reserving the excess dressing. Cook the pepper until the skin starts to blister and brown, and the flesh is tender. Alternatively, cook the pepper halves, skin side up, under a preheated hot broiler. Scrape away the charred skin and discard. Transfer the pepper halves to a serving plate and spoon the reserved dressing over them. Sprinkle with cilantro and serve with crumbled feta cheese, if liked.

Sweet potatoes are perfect for the grill because they cook quickly without pre-boiling. When tossed in dressing and wrapped in foil, the potatoes steam cook and absorb the flavors of the dressing. Care must be taken so that the potatoes do not burn through the foil where they are in direct contact with the heat. This recipe calls for individual packages, but one large package does just as well. Cook them before the meat and put them on one side of the grill to keep warm.

sesame sweet potato packages

4 large sweet potatoes, about 20 oz., peeled and cut into 4 or 5 slices
1–2 tablespoons vegetable oil
1–2 tablespoons shoyu or tamari soy sauce
1 tablespoon sesame seeds

to serve
1 tablespoon finely chopped fresh parsley

a barbecue with a lid

serves 4

Put the sweet potato in a bowl with the oil, soy sauce, and sesame seeds and toss well. Divide between 4 large squares of aluminium foil, then crinkle the foil up around them and close tightly. Put the foil packages on a preheated hot grill, close the lid and let cook for 20–30 minutes or until tender. Alternatively, place the foil packages on a baking sheet and bake in a preheated oven at 350°F for 20 minutes or until tender.

When ready to serve, open up the packages and sprinkle a little parsley on the sweet potatoes.

Note An even easier way to cook sesame sweet potatoes is to boil the potatoes for 4–5 minutes or until tender, then drain and put in a bowl. Add the soy sauce, sesame seeds, and parsley and toss well.

grilled thai pork with stir-fried noodles

This versatile Thai-inspired marinade can be used to cook any meat or fish. Like many Thai recipes, it contains a lot of ingredients, but don't be put off. A top tip is to make a double quantity and refrigerate what you don't use in a sealed container for another occasion. As many of my marinades are inspired by Oriental flavors, I often serve grilled meat and fish with noodles, but bread, rice, or potatoes are equally delicious.

18 oz. pork tenderloin, trimmed and cut into ½-inch diagonal slices

stir-fried noodles

8 oz. noodles
2-inch piece of fresh ginger, cut into 8 pieces
2 garlic cloves, halved
2 shallots, cut into 4 pieces
¼ cup grapeseed oil
1 large carrot, thinly sliced lengthways into matchsticks
1 medium leek, thinly sliced lengthways into matchsticks
½ cup hot vegetable stock

marinade

1 small piece of dried chile, to taste
1-inch piece fresh ginger, peeled
1 stick of lemon grass or grated zest of ½ unwaxed lemon
3 shallots
5 garlic cloves
1 anchovy fillet
1 tablespoon coriander seeds, crushed
1 teaspoon ground cumin
2 teaspoons cumin seeds
1 teaspoon ground turmeric
2 tablespoons shoyu or tamari soy sauce
1 tablespoon tamarind paste
1 tablespoon brown sugar
½ teaspoon sea salt
2 tablespoons olive oil

to serve

sesame oil
shoyu or tamari soy sauce
a small bunch of chives, snipped

serves 4

To make the marinade, put the ingredients in a food processor and reduce to a paste. Next, lay the slices of pork out in a single layer on a plate, then spoon over the marinade, turning the meat over so that the marinade is evenly distributed. Cover and leave for 1–24 hours to suit. (If marinating for more than 1 hour, put the pork in the refrigerator.)

When ready to cook, put the pork slices on a preheated hot grill, under a preheated hot broiler or on a stovetop grill pan. Cook the pork for 20–30 minutes on each side or until browned. Cut into one of the slices to make sure it is cooked in the middle—if it is still pink, cook for an extra 10 minutes.

Bring a large saucepan of water to the boil and cook the noodles according to the instructions on the packet. Drain the noodles in a colander, reserving half of the cooking water and returning it to the saucepan. Set the colander containing the noodles over the saucepan.

Put the ginger, garlic and shallots in a food processor and chop finely. Heat the grapeseed oil in a wok or large pan, then add the ginger mixture and stir-fry over medium heat until soft. Add the carrot and leek and stir-fry until al dente.

Pour the reserved cooking water through the noodles to prevent them sticking together, drain lightly and add to the wok. Add the stock and toss well until the vegetables are well distributed among the noodles.

Transfer the noodles to a large serving platter and drizzle generously with sesame oil and soy sauce. Arrange the pork slices on top, drizzle a little more sesame oil on the meat and sprinkle with snipped chives. Serve immediately.

Variation Try serving chicken thighs this way.

No cook-out—especially where children are involved—is complete without burgers, but burgers don't necessarily have to mean junk food. Not only is it healthier to make your own, but fun too as you can experiment with herbs and spices. This recipe can be varied to use beef, lamb, or poultry, but make sure that you use good-quality meat. The addition of bread to the mixture gives a smoother texture and flavor.

aromatic pork burger in pita bread

with chile tomato chutney

3 slices white bread
5 tablespoons milk
1¾ lb. ground pork
2 eggs
a handful of fresh parsley, finely chopped
4 garlic cloves, crushed
1 teaspoon ground cinnamon
a large pinch of ground cloves
1 teaspoon ground turmeric
a large pinch of ground red pepper
the seeds of 4 cardamom pods, crushed
1 teaspoon sea salt
freshly ground black pepper
olive oil, for brushing

yogurt dressing
10 oz. plain yogurt
the seeds of 8 cardamom pods, crushed
a large pinch of sea salt

to serve
Chile Tomato Chutney (page 15)
6 pita breads
2 cups shredded iceberg lettuce

serves 4–6

To make the yogurt dressing, put the yogurt and cardomom seeds in a small bowl, add the salt and mix well. Cover and refrigerate until required.

Soak the bread in the milk for 10–15 minutes until soft, then squeeze the bread with your hands until it is almost dry and put in a bowl. Add the ground pork, eggs, parsley, garlic, spices, salt and plenty of pepper. Mix well, cover and let stand for 60 minutes.

Shape the meat mixture into 12 patties. Cover and refrigerate until required.

When ready to cook, brush the patties lightly with olive oil and cook them on a preheated hot grill for 20 minutes, turning them from time to time to avoid burning. Cut into one of the burgers to make sure it is cooked in the middle—if it is still pink, cook for an extra 5 minutes. Alternatively, cook the burgers in a frying pan over medium heat for 20 minutes, or put them in an oiled roasting pan and cook in a preheated oven at 350°F for 20 minutes, turning from time to time. Transfer the burgers to a plate and spread each one with a spoonful of chile tomato chutney.

Heat the pita breads on the grill or in the oven until just warm. Cut each one in half, open and fill with lettuce, yogurt dressing, and a burger, then serve.

3
3

japanese teriyaki-style spareribs

Like hot dogs and hamburgers, spareribs are a must on the grill and although you can buy them in a choice of marinades, I much prefer to marinate them myself. This delicious teriyaki marinade gives the spareribs a wonderful eastern flavor and the longer you can marinate them, the better. In this recipe, the ribs are wrapped in aluminium foil and cooked slowly which makes them really succulent.

2 sides pork spareribs, about 3½ lb.

teriyaki marinade

¾ cup tamari or shoyu soy sauce
¾ cup Japanese sake or dry sherry
¾ cup mirin* or sweet sherry
¼ cup granulated sugar
freshly ground black pepper

to serve

Stir-fried Noodles (page 23)
Sesame Sweet Potato Packets (page 20)
green salad

serves 4–6

To make the teriyaki marinade, put the soy sauce, sake, mirin, and sugar in a saucepan, set over medium heat and simmer until the sugar dissolves. Set aside to cool. Put the sparerib sheets in a large freezer bag, add the marinade, seal tightly and let stand for 1–24 hours to suit, turning every now and again to allow for even distribution of the marinade. (If marinating for more than 1 hour, put the meat in the refrigerator.)

When ready to cook, drain the ribs, pouring the excess marinade into a small saucepan. Simmer the marinade over medium heat until reduced by half.

Wrap each side of spareribs in a double thickness of aluminium foil. Put the foil parcels on a preheated hot grill and cook for 15 minutes. Open the parcels, turn the meat and paint the ribs with the marinade, then close the parcels again. Repeat this 3 times or until the ribs are tender. This should take about 1 hour. To make sure the ribs are well cooked, cut into the thickest part of the meat in the center of the rib sheet with a sharp knife. If the meat is still pink, wrap the ribs up again and put them back on the barbecue for an extra 10 minutes. Once cooked, unwrap the ribs, then put them directly on the barbecue and cook on both sides to give them that special barbecue taste. Alternatively, put the marinated ribs in a roasting pan with ½ cup of cold water and cook in a preheated oven at 350°F for 60 minutes, turning once.

Transfer the sides to a cutting board and cut up the ribs. Put them on a serving platter and pour the remaining marinade over them. Serve with stir-fried noodles or sweet potato packets and a green salad.

***Note** Mirin is a sweet Japanese seasoning made from glutinous rice and is available in Asian stores and large supermarkets.

When it comes to meat, Sicily is synonymous with lamb, especially in spring. I happened to be in Palermo one Easter Sunday and, curious to know how the locals spent the day, I was told that they went into the woods to cook a roast. On our way back from lunch in a nearby town later that day, we took the scenic route through the hairpin bends of the forest-clad mountains. We were amazed to find clusters of anorak-clad *Palermitani* scattered untidily through the eucalyptus forests, clustered around camp fires, with boxes, bottles, and baskets littered everywhere and cars abandoned along the roadside. Smoke wafted in every direction and the air was heavy with the scent of roasting lamb.

sicilian-style lamb chops

with lemon and garlic marinade

2½ lb. lamb chops
6 garlic cloves, crushed
freshly squeezed juice of 2 lemons
5 tablespoons extra virgin olive oil
1 teaspoon dried oregano
1 bay leaf, torn
freshly ground black pepper

to serve
2 handfuls arugula
coarse sea salt
lemon wedges

serves 4–6

Put the lamb chops in a freezer bag, then add the garlic, lemon juice, olive oil, oregano, bay leaf, and plenty of black pepper. Seal tightly and let stand for 1–24 hours to suit, turning from time to time to allow for even distribution of the marinade. (If marinating for more than 1 hour, put the meat in the refrigerator.)

When ready to cook, drain the chops, reserving the marinade. Put the chops on a preheated hot grill, under a preheated broiler or on a hot stovetop grill pan, and cook for 20–30 minutes or until golden brown, turning the meat from time to time and basting it with the marinade as you do so. To make sure the lamb is well cooked, cut into the thickest part of the meat with a sharp knife—if still pink, cook the chops for an extra 10 minutes. Alternatively, put the marinated chops in a roasting pan with ½ cup of cold water and cook in a preheated oven at 350°F for 60 minutes, turning once. (Reserve the pan juices to pour over the lamb when serving.)

Spread the arugula over a serving dish, place the chops on top, sprinkle with salt and serve with lemon wedges.

Cooking on a grill is a skill that has to be learned through experience and roasting a whole roast does need practice to get it right. My friends Nick and Sandra grill their roast on a regular basis and Nick has developed the perfect method for cooking beef. It is dark, crusty, and smoky on the outside while succulent red rare in the middle. Nick says it is essential to choose a large, thick piece of meat weighing a minimum of 4½ pounds, as smaller, flatter pieces dry out too much. The meat should be lean, but have plenty of fat around the outside, as this will keep it moist as it cooks and will ensure more flavor. It is essential to have a grill with a lid for roasting meat.

nick's barbecued rare roast beef

1 lb. good-quality beef, such as bottom round or sirloin

a charcoal grill with a lid and a ventilator

serves 8

Prepare the charcoal as usual—briquettes are excellent for this recipe. When very hot, push the briquettes out to the side, leaving a circle of coals with a hole in the center the size of your piece of meat. Line this crater with aluminium foil, creating a "dish" underneath to catch the juices.

Place a wire grill over the coals, put the meat on top and cook for 50 minutes, turning every 10–15 minutes, until cooked evenly all over. To increase the heat, prop the lid of the barbecue open a little from time to time. Alternatively, put the beef in a roasting pan and cook in a preheated oven at 400ºF for 40 minutes. When cooked, rest the meat for 20 minutes before serving.

Note Take care when raising the lid of the grill, as the fat in the foil may ignite. Should this happen, simply replace the lid to extinguish the flame.

marinated herbed steak served panino style

with hummus, tomato, and basil

It is well worth buying your meat from a local butcher if you can—good butchers know their animals, their meat and their customers. Although asking for what you need might seem more daunting than simply picking it up in a supermarket, it is well worth the extra effort for the superior quality of meat. A decent strip of fat around the steak makes for good grilling and excellent flavor. Choose dark, red meat, lightly marbled and a moderate amount of fat along one side. Fat is essential for flavor and keeping the steak succulent—you don't have to eat it.

4 good-quality sirloin steaks, about 7 oz. each
1 large tomato, thinly sliced
1 tablespoon olive oil, plus extra for brushing
12 fresh basil leaves
4 panini or English muffins
sea salt and freshly ground black pepper
¾ cup ready-made hummus, to serve

marinade
¼ cup red wine
2 teaspoons balsamic vinegar
4 garlic cloves, crushed
a large handful of mixed fresh herbs, such as rosemary, sage, thyme, or parsley
2 tablespoons extra virgin olive oil
1 teaspoon black peppercorns, crushed

serves 4

To make the marinade, put the wine, vinegar, garlic, herbs, olive oil, and black pepper in a food processor and reduce to a paste. Put the steaks in a freezer bag, then add the marinade and seal tightly. Let stand for 1–2 hours to suit, turning the bag from time to time.

When ready to cook, remove the steak from the marinade and let drain. Brush with a little olive oil and transfer to a preheated hot grill or a preheated hot stovetop grill pan. Sear on both sides until well browned, 1–2 minutes on each side for rare meat. For medium or well-done, cook for a further 5–10 minutes, then let cool slightly.

Meanwhile, put the tomato slices on a plate, drizzle with the olive oil and season with salt and pepper. Sprinkle the basil leaves on top.

When cool enough to handle, cut the steak into slices. Cut the panini in half, and toast them on the grill or stovetop grill pan. Spread half of the panini halves with hummus, put slices of steak on top and top with the tomato and basil. Sandwich with the remaining panini halves and serve immediately.

As a general rule, I avoid cooking chicken breast. Firstly, it does not have the flavor of dark meat and, secondly, because the meat is thick and dense, it can easily become dry and stringy. The answer is to beat the flesh to between half and a third of its original thickness, as it will then cook quickly and evenly, retaining its moisture. Chinese five-spice powder is one of my favorite spice blends. Containing fennel, cinnamon, cloves, star anise, and black pepper, it is distinctive and aromatic, without being overpowering or spicy hot, and it lends itself to marinades of all kinds.

char-grilled chicken breast

with mixed leaves and balsamic dressing

4 fresh boneless chicken breasts, about 2 lb.

marinade

2 teaspoons Chinese five-spice powder
1 teaspoon ground ginger
2 tablespoons balsamic vinegar
1 tablespoon extra virgin olive oil
1 teaspoon sea salt
freshly ground black pepper

balsamic dressing

¼ cup extra virgin olive oil
2 tablespoons balsamic vinegar
1 teaspoon mustard powder
1 tablespoon freshly squeezed lemon juice
2 teaspoons sugar
sea salt and freshly ground black pepper

to serve

5 oz. mixed salad leaves, such as arugula, watercress, mâche, radicchio, or baby spinach
Sesame Sweet Potato Packets (page 20)

a ridged stovetop grill pan

serves 4

Lay a piece of plastic wrap on a cutting board, put a chicken breast in the middle and flatten it with the palms of your hands. Cover it with a second piece of plastic wrap, beat it flat with a meat cleaver, then remove the plastic wrap. Repeat with the remaining chicken breasts.

To make the marinade, put the five-spice powder, ginger, vinegar, olive oil, and salt in a small bowl, season with black pepper and mix well. Spoon this over both sides of the chicken breasts, piling them on a plate as you go. Cover and let stand for 1–24 hours to suit. (If marinating for more than 1 hour, put the chicken in the refrigerator.)

To make the balsamic dressing, put the olive oil, vinegar, mustard powder, lemon juice, and sugar in a jar, then add salt and pepper to taste, put the lid on and shake well.

When ready to cook, put the chicken on a preheated hot ridged stovetop grill pan on top of a preheated hot grill and cook on both sides until charred, about 10 minutes in total, lifting the corners from time to time to check that it is not burning. To make sure the chicken is cooked, cut into the thickest part with a sharp knife—if it is still pink, cook for a few more minutes.

Cover a large serving platter with the salad leaves. Arrange the cooked chicken breasts on top and drizzle the dressing over the chicken and the salad. Serve immediately with sesame sweet potato packets.

Like peaches and cream, seafood and hot peppers are meant for each other. The trick is to use just the right amount of chile so that it brings out the flavor of the seafood without masking it. Whole chopped chiles are aromatic when used sparingly, unlike chile powder, which tends to dominate a dish. Cooked in their shells, tiger shrimp retain their flavor and require minimum preparation. They also look fantastic and make ideal finger food.

spiked tiger shrimp

with lime and chile marinade

12 raw tiger shrimp, shell on

lime and chile marinade

finely grated zest and freshly squeezed juice of 1 unwaxed lime
2 tablespoons extra virgin olive oil
1 medium fresh chile, chopped
a large pinch of ground mace
sea salt

to serve

5 oz. mixed salad leaves, such as arugula, watercress, mâche, radicchio, or baby spinach
sea salt and freshly ground black pepper
extra virgin olive oil, for drizzling
Mango, Kiwi, and Cilantro Salsa (page 15)

12 wooden skewers, soaked overnight

serves 4

To make the marinade, put the lime zest and juice, olive oil, chile, mace, and salt in a small bowl and let stand for 5–10 minutes.

Meanwhile, insert the pointed end of the skewer into the head end of a shrimp and push it through the entire length and out the tail end so that the shrimp is straight. Lay it on a large piece of aluminium foil, then repeat with the remaining shrimp.

Rub the shrimp with the marinade, wrap them up in the foil and let marinate for 1–2 hours.

When ready to cook, open the foil parcel, lay the skewered shrimp on a preheated hot grill and cook for 5 minutes, turning once, until the shrimp turn pink. To make sure they are cooked, insert a sharp knife into a shrimp. If it is still raw, cook for a little longer. Alternatively, wrap the marinated shrimp in a large, loose parcel of foil, put on a baking sheet and cook in a preheated oven at 425°F for 5 minutes. Open the parcel and return the shrimp to the oven, uncovered, for 5 minutes.

Cover a large serving dish with the salad leaves, dress with a little salt and pepper and drizzle with olive oil. Lay the shrimp skewers across the salad and serve with mango, kiwi, and cilantro salsa.

foil-wrapped trout

with prosciutto, olives, and mushrooms

This is a very simple recipe that can be adapted to cook many types of fish, such as sea bass, sea bream, mackerel, and fillets of salmon. Very thin slices of bacon or pancetta can be used instead of prosciutto.

Clean the trout, leaving the head on. Take a piece of aluminium foil, large enough to enclose one of the fish, and grease with oil. Lay one of the fish diagonally across the middle. Put a sage leaf, a slice of prosciutto, salt and pepper inside the fish. Crinkle the foil up around the edge of the fish. Put a second sage leaf on top of the fish, then add a quarter of the mushroom slices, 3 olives, and 1 tablespoon of wine. Drizzle with olive oil and lemon juice and season with salt and pepper.

Close the foil loosely around the fish, like a pasty, and transfer to a preheated hot grill. Cook for 10–15 minutes, then let rest for 5 minutes. Alternatively, put the foil parcels on a baking sheet and cook in a preheated oven at 425°F for 15–20 minutes. Serve in the parcels with new potatoes and a tomato and basil salad.

4 medium-sized trout or 2 large trout fillets, 2–2½ lb.
8 fresh sage leaves or sprigs of thyme
4 slices of prosciutto or thinly sliced bacon
8 small mushrooms, thinly sliced
12 small green olives
¼ cup white wine
4 teaspoons olive oil, plus extra for greasing
freshly squeezed juice of 1 lemon
sea salt and freshly ground black pepper

to serve
new potatoes
tomato and basil salad

serves 4

This makes a wonderful vegetarian grilling option, as well as a tasty side dish or a appetizer for all. Bagna cauda, literally meaning warm bath, is an important part of the traditional food of the Piedmont region of Italy and is traditionally served fondue-style with cooked or raw vegetables. Every mountain valley has its own version. The ingredients are cooked over a low flame, creating a velvety sauce that can be served as a dip or poured over the season's vegetables.

vegetables kabobs

with bagna cauda dressing

vegetable kabobs

1 ear corn-on-the-cob, husked and cut into 8 pieces
1 red bell pepper, deseeded and cut into 8 pieces
8 mushroom caps
1 yellow bell pepper, deseeded and cut into 8 pieces
4 small onions
sea salt and freshly ground black pepper
vegetable oil, for brushing

bagna cauda dressing

3 garlic cloves
1½ oz. salted anchovy fillets, rinsed and dried
2 tablespoons butter
½ cup walnut or olive oil

4 metal skewers

serves 4

To make the dressing, grind the garlic and anchovies to a paste using a mortar and pestle. Put a small pan over very low heat and melt the butter. Add the garlic and anchovy paste and stir well until the paste dissolves in the butter. Add the walnut oil and simmer for 10 minutes, whisking the mixture continuously.

Thread a piece of corn onto a skewer, followed by a piece of red pepper, a mushroom, a piece of yellow pepper and an onion. Continue threading the vegetables, this time in reverse order, finishing with a piece of corn. Repeat with the remaining skewers and ingredients.

Brush the kabobs with vegetable oil and sprinkle with salt and pepper. Cook on a preheated hot grill or under a hot broiler for 20–30 minutes until tender, turning from time to time. Transfer to plates, pour the dressing over the kabobs, then serve.

families outdoors

We all love to be outside because it offers a breathing space for everybody. Family life revolves around mealtimes; even more so out of doors as the fresh air makes everyone hungry. This chapter is full of recipes and ideas for breakfast, brunch, lunch, afternoon tea, and supper. It features simple snacks, rich salad meals, sweet treats, and satisfying pasta dishes and pies for adults and children alike to enjoy.

Bruschetta toppings are easy to make and very versatile. Many work well stirred into pasta or rice, or blended to make a dip. Here are two recipes that make a delicious appetizer or light lunch. The first is an update on the classic mozzarella, tomato, and basil salad, which originally came from the island of Capri, off the coast of Italy. In the second recipe, I have simply crushed the beans so that they still have texture, but they can also be puréed to a hummus-like consistency. Try experimenting with different combinations of pulses, herbs, and spices.

bruschetta with baby mozzarella, cherry tomatoes, and arugula

8 oz. baby mozzarellas, drained and halved
2 cups cherry tomatoes, halved
¼ cup good-quality extra virgin olive oil, plus extra to serve
1 ciabatta loaf, left out overnight to dry out, if possible
1 large garlic clove, unpeeled and halved
1 handful arugula
sea salt and freshly ground black pepper
balsamic vinegar, to serve

a ridged stovetop grill pan (optional)

serves 4

Put the mozzarella and tomatoes in a large bowl, add the olive oil, season with plenty of salt and pepper and mix well. Cover and leave to marinate for 1–2 hours.

When ready to serve, slice the bread open lengthways and toast both sides on a preheated ridged stovetop grill pan over medium–high heat. Alternatively, toast the bread under a preheated medium broiler. Rub the toasted sides with the garlic and drizzle with olive oil. Toss the arugula with the mozzarella and tomato and spoon onto the toasted bread. Drizzle with balsamic vinegar and serve immediately.

bruschetta with crushed butter beans and lemon dressing

1½ cups dried butter beans, soaked overnight, or 14-oz. can butter beans, drained
1 ciabatta loaf, left out overnight to dry out, if possible
1 large garlic clove, unpeeled and halved

lemon dressing
6 salted anchovy fillets, rinsed and dried
a large handful of fresh parsley
grated zest and freshly squeezed juice of 1 unwaxed lemon
¼ cup extra virgin olive oil
1 garlic clove
3½ oz. pancetta or thick-sliced bacon, finely chopped
½ cup dry white wine
freshly ground black pepper

to serve
extra virgin olive oil
finely chopped fresh parsley

a ridged stovetop grill pan (optional)

serves 4

If using dried beans, rinse and place in a large saucepan with plenty of water. Bring to the boil, then simmer for 30–60 minutes until tender—the cooking time will depend on the freshness of the beans so taste before draining.

To make the lemon dressing, put the anchovies, parsley, and lemon zest on a cutting board and chop together finely. Put the olive oil and garlic in a small saucepan and cook over very low heat. When the garlic starts to color, discard it, increase the heat to medium and add the pancetta and the anchovy mixture. Add some black pepper and fry for 3 minutes, stirring continuously. Add the lemon juice and wine and cook over low heat for 5 minutes, stirring from time to time. Add the beans and cook for a few more minutes, stirring. Crush the beans with a potato masher to break them up a little.

Slice the bread open lengthways and toast both sides on a preheated ridged stovetop grill pan over medium–high heat. Alternatively, toast the bread under a preheated medium broiler. Cut the bread in half, then rub the toasted sides with the garlic and drizzle with olive oil. Spoon the beans on top and sprinkle with olive oil and parsley. Serve immediately.

Although adding vinegar to the poaching water will help keep the white of the egg together, the only way to make a good poached egg is to use fresh free-range eggs from a local source, if possible. No other way of cooking an egg tests the quality and freshness quite so much. The richness of the yolk, the freshness of the asparagus and the subtle saltiness of the pancetta is a heavenly combination.

bruschetta with asparagus, pancetta, and poached egg

1 bunch of asparagus, trimmed (8–12 spears)
4 teaspoons butter, melted
½ nutmeg, plus extra to serve
8 thin slices of pancetta, about 2½ oz.
1 tablespoon vinegar
4 eggs
1 ciabatta loaf, left out overnight to dry out, if possible
1 large garlic clove, unpeeled and halved
extra virgin olive oil, to serve

a ridged stovetop grill pan (optional)

serves 4

Cook the asparagus in a saucepan of lightly salted boiling water until tender. Drain carefully, taking care not to break the tips. Transfer to a plate and pour the melted butter over the asparagus, reserving a little, then grate the nutmeg on top. Keep the plate warm.

Fry the pancetta in a dry nonstick frying pan until the slices start to crinkle and brown. Turn and brown on the other side.

Heat a shallow saucepan of water until the water is simmering and add the vinegar. Crack open the eggs, drop them one at a time into the water and cook according to taste, 1 minute for a soft poached egg. Lift the eggs out with a slotted spoon and transfer to a plate, carefully draining off any excess water as you do so.

Cut the ciabatta open lengthways and toast both sides on a preheated ridged stovetop grill pan over medium–high heat. Alternatively, toast the bread under a preheated medium broiler. Cut each piece of ciabatta in half crossways, rub the toasted sides of the bread lightly with the garlic and drizzle with olive oil.

Put 2 slices of pancetta on each piece of ciabatta, lay the asparagus across the pancetta and place a poached egg on top. Spoon the remaining melted butter over the top and grate over a little extra nutmeg. Serve immediately.

The combination of chicken livers, mushrooms, and bacon makes a delicious pâté that freezes well, so it's a good idea to make a double quantity and freeze what you don't use. Spoon the pâté into ramekins before freezing so that you have small portions ready to serve. If you prefer a smooth pâté, blend the ingredients in a food processor until smooth.

chicken liver, mushroom, and bacon crostini

1 oz. dried porcini mushrooms
8 oz. chicken livers, rinsed and dried
6 oz. button mushrooms, quartered
4 slices thick-sliced bacon, cut into 4–5 pieces
12 tablespoons (1½ sticks) lightly salted butter, plus extra for spreading
1 bay leaf, plus extra to serve
1 tablespoon fresh thyme or ½ teaspoon dried thyme
2 baguettes, left out overnight to dry out, if possible
warmed milk, for soaking
sea salt (optional) and freshly ground black pepper
extra virgin olive oil, for drizzling

makes about 48

Put the porcini mushrooms and milk in a bowl and soak for the length of time detailed in the instructions on the packet. Squeeze the mushrooms to get rid of the excess liquid and transfer to a small saucepan. Add the chicken livers, button mushrooms, bacon, butter, herbs, and a good grinding of black pepper. Put the saucepan over medium heat and allow the butter to melt, then stir well and cover. Cook for 10 minutes, then transfer to a food processor and chop roughly. Taste and add salt, if necessary.

Cut the baguette into diagonal slices, ½ inch thick and spread with butter and a thick layer of the chicken liver mixture. Arrange on 2 baking sheets and drizzle with olive oil. Cook in a preheated oven at 425ºF for 10 minutes or until the bread is crisp. Serve immediately on platters decorated with bay leaves.

It is now possible to buy a good range of quality beans in cans and they all lend themselves well to this recipe. Tangy sun-dried tomatoes work well with the richness of beans and the best ones to use are sun-dried tomatoes preserved in oil. You can use dried ones, but you must soak them first or they will be hard and chewy.

chickpea and sun-dried tomato crostini

1 14-oz. can chickpeas, drained
a handful of fresh parsley, chopped, plus extra to serve
6 sun-dried tomato halves preserved in oil, drained and finely chopped
1 tablespoon olive oil, plus extra to serve
1 baguette, left out overnight to dry out, if possible
2 garlic cloves, unpeeled and halved
sea salt and freshly ground black pepper

makes about 24

Mash the chickpeas well, add the parsley, sun-dried tomatoes, and olive oil and mix well. Add salt and pepper to taste.

Cut the baguette into diagonal slices ½ inch thick, arrange on a baking sheet and bake in a preheated oven at 424°F until really crisp and dry.

Rub the toasts with the garlic and sprinkle with salt. Pile the chickpea mixture on the toast, sprinkle with parsley and drizzle with olive oil. Serve immediately.

This Catalan salad is a refreshing change from the more usual *Salade Niçoise*. The serrano ham makes for an altogether more savory dish and the formal arrangement of the ingredients on a platter, as opposed to being chopped up in a salad bowl, looks stunning. Aioli is a Catalan favorite and is also delicious served with raw or cooked vegetables.

catalan salad

with tuna and aioli

3½ oz. thin green beans (haricots verts)
2 heads baby romaine lettuces
3½ oz. thinly sliced serrano ham or prosciutto
4 hard-cooked eggs, halved lengthways
6½ oz. good-quality canned tuna, drained and broken into large chunks
8 large pitted green olives, halved
2 tablespoons extra virgin olive oil
2 tablespoons sherry or red wine vinegar
sea salt and freshly ground black pepper

aioli

4 garlic cloves, unpeeled
½ teaspoon salt
2 teaspoons freshly squeezed lemon juice
1 egg yolk
¾ cup extra virgin olive oil

serves 4

To make the aioli, put the garlic cloves in a mortar and bash them lightly with a pestle, pulling away the skin as it frees itself. Add the salt and grind the garlic to a smooth paste. Transfer to a large, wide bowl, add the lemon juice and the egg yolk and whisk with a metal whisk. Continue whisking as you add the olive oil a few drops at a time; as the aioli starts to thicken, add the oil in a slow, steady stream. This should take about 5 minutes. If you prefer a lighter mayonnaise, whisk in 2 tablespoons of boiling water. Transfer to a serving bowl, cover and chill until required.

Cook the beans in salted boiling water for 3–4 minutes until al dente, then drain and plunge into ice water. Drain and dry. Cover a large platter with lettuce leaves, then fan the beans around the rim of the platter, sticking out from under the edge of the lettuce leaves. Twist the slices of serrano ham and arrange them on the lettuce leaves, then arrange the eggs, tuna, and olive halves on top. Drizzle the olive oil and vinegar over the salad, then add salt and pepper. Serve with the aioli in a separate bowl.

Variation Use chicken breasts instead of tuna.

The combination of colors and textures in this salad is a knockout. It can be made with other beans, but black beans work particularly well, as they highlight the colors of the other ingredients. Rather than cooking just enough beans for your recipe, cook a whole packet and freeze what you don't use in small containers. The texture does not deteriorate and they are a useful salad ingredient to have on hand.

herbed black bean and avocado salad

1 cup dried black beans, soaked overnight or 2 15-oz cans black beans, drained
1 14-oz can corn, drained
1 large red bell pepper, deseeded and diced
a handful of fresh parsley, finely chopped
a handful of mixed fresh herbs, such as basil, mint, dill, or fennel fronds, finely chopped
3 tablespoons extra virgin olive oil
1 avocado
1 tablespoon freshly squeezed lemon juice
sea salt and freshly ground black pepper

serves 4

If using dried beans, rinse, then put in a large saucepan with plenty of water. Bring to the boil, then simmer for 30–60 minutes or until tender and drain.

Put the beans in a large salad bowl and add the corn, red pepper, herbs, and olive oil. Stir well and cover until required.

When ready to serve, peel and pit the avocado, then cut into small cubes and put in a small bowl. Add the lemon juice, season with salt and pepper and mix well. Add the avocado to the bean salad and mix well. Taste and add more salt and pepper, if necessary, then serve.

Everybody loves potato salad and it is also a great way of using up excess cooked new potatoes. That said, the best potato salad is made while the potatoes are still warm. The flavor of the mayonnaise and other ingredients permeates the potato, giving a richer, rounder taste.

new potato, smoked turkey, and chive salad

3 lb. boiling potatoes
7 oz. good-quality wafer-thin smoked turkey
1 cup mayonnaise
6 large green pitted olives, finely chopped
a handful of fresh chives or fennel fronds, finely snipped, plus extra to serve
chive flowers, to serve (optional)

serves 4

Put the potatoes in a large pan of salted water, then bring to the boil and simmer until tender. Drain and leave until cool enough to handle. Meanwhile, cut half of the turkey into slivers and put in a large bowl with the mayonnaise, olives, and chives. Cut the potatoes in half, add to the bowl, then mix well and transfer to a serving platter.

Roll up the remaining slices of turkey and arrange them around the outside of the potatoes. Sprinkle with chives, decorate with chive flowers, if liked, and serve.

Pasta is a great standby meal—quick to cook and always a favorite with kids. Its versatile nature means that you can throw just about anything from the store cupboard or the refrigerator in with it, whether it be vegetables, meat, or fish. All you need to do then is add some homemade tomato sauce or béchamel, mix it and bake it in the oven. That is exactly how this recipe came about—it went down so well that the only problem was recreating it.

potluck summer pasta

2 tablespoons coarse sea salt
16 oz. penne or rigatoni
1 28-oz. can Italian plum tomatoes, drained and deseeded
6 garlic cloves, lightly crushed
1 teaspoon dried oregano or 1 small piece of chile, to taste
1 cup cooked peas, corn or sliced mushrooms
12 oz. canned tuna in oil, half drained
3½ oz. cooked ham or chicken, cut into slivers
1 tablespoon salted capers, rinsed, dried, and chopped
5 oz. mozzarella cheese, diced
2 oz. salami, finely chopped (optional)
15 g crisp breadcrumbs*
extra virgin olive oil, for frying and drizzling

béchamel sauce
3 tablespoons butter
¼ cup flour
1¾ cup warmed milk
freshly grated nutmeg
sea salt

serves 4

Bring a 5-quart saucepan of water to the boil, add the salt and the pasta and cook over high heat until slightly less than al dente. Drain the pasta, reserving 2 tablespoons of the cooking water, and return to the saucepan.

Meanwhile, cover the base of a medium saucepan with olive oil. Put over high heat, and when the oil is searing hot, add the tomatoes. Cook for 1–2 minutes, taking care not to burn the tomatoes, but allowing them to caramelize a little. Reduce the heat and mash the tomatoes with a potato masher, then add the garlic and oregano. Stir well, cover and cook for a few minutes, then add the mushrooms, if using, cover and cook for 20 minutes. Stir in the tuna, capers, peas, and ham and heat through.

To make the béchamel sauce, melt the butter in a small saucepan, and when it starts to bubble, add the flour and mix well. Cook over gentle heat for 1–2 minutes, then whisk in the milk and continue cooking until the sauce thickens. Add grated nutmeg and salt to taste.

Add the sauce to the pasta with the reserved water and mix until the pasta is well coated. Stir in the mozzarella and salami, if using. Transfer to a large, shallow buttered ovenproof dish and pour the béchamel sauce over the top. Sprinkle with the breadcrumbs. Drizzle with olive oil and bake in a preheated oven at 425°F for 20–30 minutes until golden. Serve immediately.

***Note** To make crisp breadcrumbs, cut the crusts off a large, slightly stale, white loaf and lay them on a large baking sheet. Bake in a preheated oven at 200°F for about 1 hour until they have dried out completely and are crisp all the way through. Let cool, break into large pieces, then put in a food processor and reduce to fine crumbs. Store in an airtight tin lined with a freezer bag and use as required. To make soft breadcrumbs, cut the remaining bread into large chunks, put in a food processor and reduce to fine crumbs. Transfer to a freezer bag, then store in the freezer and use as required.

This simple recipe is ideal for family meals or any unexpected guests and it's worth having some good-quality Italian-made dried pasta in your store cupboard for such occasions. Boil the pasta in 10 quarts of rapidly boiling water with a good handful of added salt. Follow the cooking time on the package, tasting it 2 minutes before the suggested time is up.

penne with mascarpone, spinach, and pancetta

- 5 oz. pancetta, diced
- 1 garlic clove, finely chopped
- 16 oz. penne
- 6 oz. mascarpone cheese
- 1 cup freshly grated Parmesan cheese, plus extra to serve
- 6 oz. young spinach leaves, washed and dried
- sea salt and freshly ground black pepper

serves 4

Heat a large frying pan over medium heat for a few minutes. Add the pancetta and garlic and cook until the fat runs and the pancetta is crispy and golden.

Bring a large saucepan of salted water to the boil, add the pasta and cook according to the instructions on the packet. Drain, reserving 4 tablespoons of the cooking water, and return to the saucepan.

Meanwhile, put the mascarpone in a small saucepan, add the reserved water and heat through gently. Add to the pasta with the Parmesan and a generous grinding of black pepper, and stir well.

Add the spinach and garlic and pancetta, including the fat from the frying pan, and stir well. Serve immediately with Parmesan.

Variation You can vary the vegetables—try arugula or lightly cooked leeks, peas, fava beans, haricots verts, or carrots.

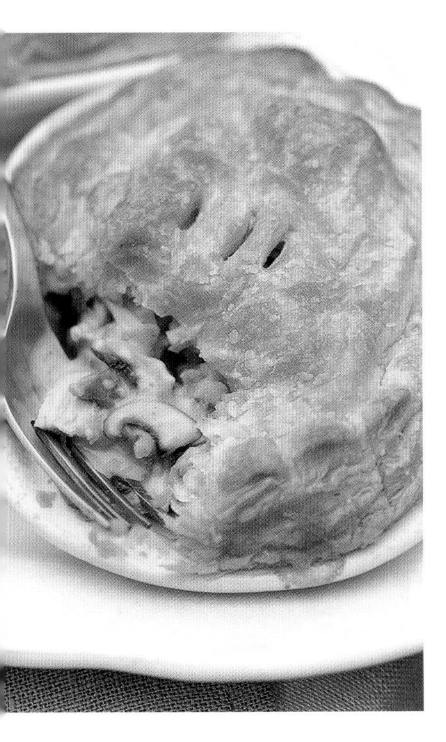

Pies such as these are family favorites in our house. Small pies are great to take on picnics. You can vary the fillings according to your family's likes and dislikes. Try using peas or haricots verts instead of mushrooms, turkey instead of chicken, and fresh tomato sauce instead of the béchamel sauce.

chicken, ham, and mushroom pies

If using a whole chicken, put it in a roasting pan and season with salt and pepper, then cook it in a preheated oven at 400°F for 1 hour. Remove from the oven and let cool. Increase the oven temperature to 425°F.

When the chicken is cool enough to handle, transfer to a cutting board and reserve the roasting pan with the chicken juices for later use. Pull the skin off the chicken and discard. Pull the chicken meat off the bones, cut into bite-sized strips and transfer to the pie dish.

Set the roasting pan of chicken juices, or butter if using ready-cooked chicken, over medium heat. Add the mushrooms, salt, and pepper and cook for 5 minutes or until the mushrooms are tender. Add the flour and stir well, add the warmed milk and continue to cook and stir until the sauce thickens. Add the slivers of ham and stir again. Divide the sauce among the pie dishes and let cool a little.

Roll out the puff pastry into a 12–13 inch square. Cut out 4 circles the same size as the pie dishes. Brush the rims of the pie dishes with cold water, then lay the pastry lids on top, pressing the pastry edges together firmly around the rim. Brush the pastry lids with water and make several small cuts in the middle of the pastry.

Put the pies on a baking sheet and bake in the center of the oven, preheated to 425°F if not previously used to cook the chicken, for 20–25 minutes. Serve with new potatoes tossed in butter and mint, your choice of vegetables and Dijon mustard, if liked.

Variation Instead of using cooked chicken and ham, stir 10 oz. raw cubed cod and 10 oz. salmon and 5 oz. cooked peeled shrimp into the hot béchamel sauce.

one 3½ lb. whole chicken or 1 lb. freshly cooked chicken meat
50 g butter (optional)
6 oz. mushrooms, thinly sliced
¼ cup flour
1¾ cups whole milk, warmed
3½ oz. cooked ham, cut into slivers
8 oz. ready-made puff pastry
sea salt and freshly ground black pepper

to serve
new potatoes tossed in butter and chopped fresh mint
cooked vegetables, such as green beans, carrots, zucchini, or brocolli
Dijon mustard (optional)

4 small pie dishes, about 5 inches diameter

serves 4–6

This recipe is based on the French classic upside-down apple tart, *tarte des demoiselles Tatin*, and makes a great summer vegetarian lunch, supper dish, or appetizer. I have used the classic Tatin pastry, but if you are in a hurry, use 8 ounces ready-made puff pastry, which makes an excellent substitute.

caramelized vegetable tarte tatin

6 tablespoons butter
1 large red bell pepper, deseeded and cut into 12 wedges
1 large yellow bell pepper, deseeded and cut into 12 wedges
1 large fennel bulb or 2 large onions, cut into 12 wedges
2 small eggplants or 2 trimmed leeks, sliced lengthways into 8 pieces and halved crossways
4 garlic cloves, crushed
1 teaspoon fresh thyme leaves
sea salt and freshly ground black pepper

pastry
1¾ cups flour
a pinch of sea salt
10 tablespoons softened butter
1 tablespoon confectioners' sugar
2 egg yolks

to serve
1 tablespoon fresh snipped chives or fennel fronds
tomato and arugula salad

a tarte tatin dish or a heavy-based flameproof ovenproof dish, 8–10 inches diameter

serves 4 as entrée or 8 as appetizer

To make the pastry, put the flour, salt, butter, sifted confectioners' sugar, and egg yolks in a large bowl. Mix quickly with your hands to form a soft dough. Wrap in plastic wrap and chill in the coldest part of the refrigerator for about 30 minutes.

Meanwhile, heat the tarte tatin dish over high heat, reduce the heat, then add the butter and heat until it has melted. Arrange the vegetable wedges like spokes on a wheel, alternating the peppers, fennel, and eggplant, until the dish is full. Season with salt and pepper, and add the garlic and thyme leaves. Cook until tender and caramelized around the edges, jiggling the vegetables with a wooden spatula from time to time so that they cook evenly.

Roll out the pastry to a circle ½–¾ inch thick to fit the pan snugly. Put it on top of the vegetables and press down firmly. Prick all over with a fork. Transfer to a preheated oven and bake at 400°F for 20–30 minutes until golden.

Run a knife around the edge of the pastry to loosen it, then put a large ovenproof platter face down on the top of the pan. Holding the platter and pan together, invert quickly, giving it a good sharp shake as you do so, onto the plate. Set aside to rest so that the caramelized vegetable juices soak into the pastry.

When ready to serve, remove the tarte tatin dish, sprinkle with chives and serve warm with a tomato and arugula salad.

carpaccio of cantaloupe
with raspberry sauce

Raspberry purée makes the perfect accompaniment to many fruits. More tangy than strawberry, it has a distinctive flavor and the color looks spectacular on the plate. This vesatile dish works equally well as a dessert or a appetizer. Alternatively, try adding smoked salmon for the perfect breakfast or brunch treat.

1 pint raspberries
¼ cup confectioners' sugar, plus extra to dust
1 cantaloupe
freshly ground black pepper
4 sprigs of mint or sweet cicely, to serve

serves 4

Set aside 8 perfect raspberries and put the remaining raspberries in a food processor. Add the confectioners' sugar. Transfer to a fine sieve set over a bowl, then push through with the back of a wooden spoon.

Cut the melon into 8 wedges, discard the seeds and cut off the skin. Slice the wedges into very thin slices and arrange on individual plates or a serving platter with the raspberries. Dust lightly with black pepper and confectioners' sugar, then cover and chill.

When ready to serve, spoon the raspberry purée over the melon, creating a pattern of lines over the fruit and the plate. Decorate with sprigs of mint.

fruit platter
with spiced caramel

Tropical and summer fruits are so luscious that they need little or no help from the cook to improve them. However, there are simple ways to serve them that give them an edge. A spiced caramel enhances and enriches the flavor of the fruit and, drizzled on the fruit in lines or spots, makes for a stunning dish.

8 oz. thinly sliced melon, mango, kiwi fruit, or pineapple, or halved peaches, apricots, or strawberries
1 cup granulated sugar
3 tablespoons water
1 teaspoon ground aniseed or cinnamon
sprigs of mint or sweet cicely, to serve

serves 4

Arrange the fruit on individual plates or a large platter. Put the sugar, water, and aniseed in a small saucepan, place over high heat and boil without stirring until it starts to change color and has a thick and syrupy appearance.

Spoon the caramel over the fruit in a fine stream or in spots, creating a pattern over the fruit and the plate. Top with mint sprigs, then serve, with any leftover spiced caramel in a separate jug.

fruit fool

1 lb. blueberries, or rhubarb (cut into 2-inch pieces), or plums, halved and pitted
½–⅓ cup granulated sugar, to taste

custard
1 cup milk
1 vanilla bean
2 egg yolks
1 tablespoon granulated sugar
2 teaspoons cornstarch

to serve
½ cup cream (optional)
fresh mint leaves (optional)

serves 4–6

Fruit fools are the epitome of English country summer food and are the perfect way to enjoy acidic fruit, such as blueberries, rhubarb, plums, plumcots and blackberries. To save time, you can use cream instead of the custard—simply mix it into the cooked rhubarb before pouring into the glasses.

To make the custard, put the milk in a small saucepan with the vanilla bean and bring slowly to simmering point. Remove the vanilla pod, rinse, dry and put to one side. Whisk the egg yolks in a bowl with the sugar and cornstarch and slowly add the warmed milk, whisking as you do so. Strain the mixture back into the saucepan and stir continuously over low heat with a wire whisk until the mixture thickens. Pour into a clean shallow bowl to cool.

Put the blueberries in a saucepan. Add the sugar, to taste, cover and cook over low heat for 5 minutes or until tender. Transfer to a food processor and reduce to a smooth purée. When cool, transfer to a bowl and stir in the custard. Spoon into tumblers and chill until required.

When ready to serve, pour a thin layer of cream over the surface and top each one with a mint leaf, if liked.

Variation For breakfast, use plain yogurt instead of custard and serve topped with your favorite granola.

There is no quicker nor more simple recipe for a tea-time or breakfast treat than Scotch pancakes. Be warned, however, that you will have the family queueing up to eat them, so it's just as well to make a double quantity if they are hungry. Scotch pancakes should be served warm, more or less straight from the pan, spread with butter and sprinkled with sugar.

scotch pancakes

with butter and sugar

¾ cup self-rising flour
a pinch of salt
1 egg
2 tablespoons granulated sugar, plus extra to serve
½ cup milk
3 tablespoons butter, plus extra to serve

makes 12–15

Put the flour and salt in a large mixing bowl, make a well in the center and add the egg, sugar and milk. Melt 2 tablespoons of the butter in a small saucepan, then add to the mixing bowl. Work the mixture together with a wire whisk or wooden spoon to make a smooth batter. Beat for 1 minute, then set aside for 10 minutes.

Set a heavy-based frying pan or griddle over medium heat, add the remaining butter and when it melts, swish it around the pan, then pour off the excess into a small heatproof bowl. Put the pan back on the heat and spoon 1 tablespoon of the batter into the pan—this will naturally form a small, circular pancake. Cook until the pancake browns and bubbles appear on the surface, then turn it over using a palette knife or fish slice. Remove onto a warm tea towel and wrap loosely to keep warm. Cook the remaining pancake mixture in batches, returning a little of the melted butter back to the pan as necessary.

Serve immediately, spread with butter and sprinkled with sugar.

Variation For small children, make Mickey or Minnie Mouse pancakes. Spoon 1 tablespoon of the pancake mixture into the center of a heavy-based hot frying pan, then dot 2 teaspoons of pancake mixture close to the edge of the circle to form ear shapes.

***Pain au chocolat* has really taken off outside France over the last 20 years, but less well known are Italian savory *cornetti* (croissants), stuffed with mozzarella and prosciutto or cooked ham. I used to eat them for breakfast in a Roman bar close to the Pantheon on my way to work every morning. Now, back in the UK, I am forced to make my own with a pack of instant croissant dough.**

instant savory croissants

1 package of ready-to-bake croissant dough
4 paper-thin slices of cooked ham or prosciutto
1 teaspoon dried oregano
1 teaspoon sun-dried tomato paste
5 oz. mozzarella or Emmenthal cheese
freshly ground black pepper

makes 8

Open the croissant dough following the instructions on the package. Lay the sheets of dough on a work surface.

Cut each slice of ham into 2 triangles. Put a triangle of ham on each triangle of dough, sprinkle with a little oregano and black pepper and add a tiny blob of sun-dried tomato paste. Put a strip of mozzarella on the long edge of the triangle and roll the dough around the cheese, bending the roll to form a crescent shape. Transfer to a baking sheet and cook in a preheated oven at 350°F for 10 minutes or until golden. Serve warm.

Variation Try anchovy fillets instead of ham or, for a vegetarian version, replace the ham with chopped tomato.

grannie's scones

with whipped cream and strawberries

My mother's scones were the best. I'm not even sure they should be called scones, as they are different from everybody else's—they are more cake than bread, with a crumbly texture and a golden color. She used to make them just before we got home from school and they would be cooling on a wire rack, ready to split open and fill with butter and jam and take outside into the garden.

1½ cups self-rising flour
1 teaspoon baking soda
1 teaspoon cream of tartar
a pinch of salt
2 tablespoons chilled butter, diced
2 tablespoons granulated sugar
2 eggs
5–7 tablespoons sour milk

to serve
strawberry jam
½ cup whipped cream
small strawberries
confectioners' sugar

straight-sided scone cutter, 2½ inches diameter

makes 8

Sieve the flour, baking soda, cream of tartar and salt into a mixing bowl. Add the butter and rub it into the flour evenly with your fingertips, then mix in the sugar. Add 1 of the eggs and the milk and, using a knife, work the dough into a ball quickly and lightly. The dough should be soft, moist and malleable.

Transfer the dough to a floured work surface, then flatten it with your hands and shape into a circle, about 1 inch thick. If the dough is too moist, add a little extra flour. Cut out as many scones as the dough allows. Roll the trimmings into a ball, flatten it and cut out a couple more scones. Shape the remaining trimmings into 1 single scone. Transfer the scones to a baking sheet. Beat the remaining egg in a small bowl, then brush the scones with it. Bake in a preheated oven at 400ºF for 10–15 minutes until well risen and golden.

While still warm, split the scones open, spread with jam, add a spoon of whipped cream and top with a strawberry. Sprinkle with sifted confectioners' sugar.

picnics

A day in the open air is an exhilarating way to unwind. Pack up everything you need and escape to your favorite place and do nothing but luxuriate in the great outdoors all day. Take plenty to eat—dips, vegetables sticks, and filled loaves are easy and filling options and seasonal fare, like cherries, are perfect to nibble on. For a memorable feast, take a tart or pie straight from the oven and bake a cake or muffins to have with a flask of tea in the afternoon.

3 tablespoons butter
2 onions, finely chopped
a handful of fresh parsley, finely chopped
1 28-oz. can tomatoes, drained, deseeded, and chopped
1 lb. small zucchini, sliced
a handful of fresh basil leaves, chopped
10 asparagus spears, trimmed
3 eggs
5 tablespoons heavy cream
¾ cup Parmesan cheese, grated
sea salt and freshly ground black pepper

pastry
1¼ cups flour
2 tablespoons cornstarch
1½ tablespoons confectioners' sugar
a pinch of salt
5½ tablespoons butter, softened
2 small egg yolks
1 tablespoon dry white wine or ice water

a loose-based tart tin, 10 inches diameter, greased
a circle of baking parchment, 13 inches diameter

serves 6–8

primavera tart

Primavera is Italian for spring and is often used to describe risottos and pasta sauces made with a selection of early summer vegetables. I have used zucchini, tomato, and asparagus enhanced with fresh basil, but chopped baby carrots, peas, fava beans and green beans would work well. Because asparagus is delicate and looks good, I have cooked it separately and put it on top of the filling, but you could use paper-thin strips of pancetta instead.

To make the pastry, put the flours, sifted confectioners' sugar and salt in a bowl, then add the butter, egg yolks, and wine. Quickly and lightly knead the ingredients together into a smooth ball. Wrap in plastic wrap and chill in the refrigerator for 1 hour.

Meanwhile, to make the filling, melt the butter in a heavy-based frying pan, then add the onion and parsley and cook until the onion is soft, without allowing it to color. Add the tomatoes and cook for 10 minutes, then add the zucchini, basil, salt, and pepper and stir-fry for 3 minutes or until the zucchini are tender but still firm. Let cool.

Sprinkle a clean work surface and rolling pin with plenty of flour. Set the pastry in the center of the flour, then flatten it with the palm of your hand and shape it into a neat circle. Take the rolling pin and roll the pastry one way, then give it a quarter turn and roll it the other way, shaping the dough back into a circle with your hands from time to time. Continue until the pastry is about 1½ inches larger than the tart tin.

Roll the pastry loosely around the rolling pin and transfer it carefully to the greased tin. Open it out and smooth it to line the tin, pressing it into the corners. Put the baking parchment on top and fill with the baking beans. Bake in a preheated oven at 425°C for 10 minutes. Remove the baking beans and the parchment, then reduce the oven temperature to 350°C.

Meanwhile, cook the asparagus in salted boiling water for about 10 minutes until tender. The cooking time will depend on the quality of the asparagus, so taste before draining.

Pour the zucchini mixture into the pastry case and spread evenly. Arrange the asparagus tips on top, like spokes on a wheel, with the tips pointing outwards. Put the eggs, cream, Parmesan, and plenty of salt and pepper in a small bowl and whisk well. Pour over the zucchini mixture and return to the oven for 20 minutes.

If you are going on a picnic immediately, let cool slightly in the tin, wrap in aluminium foil and transfer to a picnic box. Otherwise, let cool competely, wrap in foil and refrigerate until required. Don't forget to take a pie knife and plate.

Of all the pies in this section, this is the simplest and quickest to make, and probably looks and tastes the most exotic. I used a jar of ready-made pesto, but if you make your own pesto it will be even more delicious. I first made it as an Easter treat and it went down so well that it has since become a firm favorite for festive occasions and picnics. It also works well with white fish instead of salmon.

layered salmon, shrimp, and potato filo pie

1 lb. new potatoes
1 28-oz can Italian plum tomatoes, drained, deseeded, and chopped
2 garlic cloves, crushed
1 small piece of dried chile, to taste
1 lb. salmon fillet, skin removed, cut lengthways into medium-sized chunks
½–¾ cup ready-made basil pesto
6½ tablespoons butter, melted
6 large sheets of filo pastry
6½ oz. cooked peeled shrimp
sea salt and freshly ground black pepper
olive oil, for frying
green salad, to serve

a springform cake pan, 9 inch diameter

serves 6–8

Cook the potatoes in salted boiling water for 15–20 minutes or until tender, drain and let cool.

Heat enough olive oil to cover the base of a large saucepan over medium heat. Add the tomatoes, garlic, and chile, reduce the heat to low, then cover and simmer for 30 minutes, stirring from time to time to ensure the sauce does not stick. Mash the tomatoes to a pulp using a potato masher. Season the salmon with salt and pepper, then add to the saucepan for 1–2 minutes to lightly cook. Transfer the sauce to a bowl and let cool. Slice the potatoes lengthways, then put in a bowl with the pesto and toss to coat evenly.

Brush the base and sides of the springform pan with a little of the melted butter. Brush a sheet of filo pastry with melted butter and lay it across the pan to line the base and sides of the pan, leaving any excess hanging over the sides. Brush another sheet of filo pastry with butter and lay it at right angles to the first sheet, smoothing it down to line the base and sides of the pan. There should now be an equal overhang of filo all the way round the pan. Repeat with the remaining sheets of pastry, reserving a little of the butter.

Cover the base of the pie with half the potato mixture, followed by half the sauce and half the shrimp. Make a second layer of each and then carefully fold the overhang of pastry over the filling. Brush the top of the pie with the remaining melted butter.

Set the pan on a baking sheet and cook in a preheated oven at 400°F for 25 minutes until golden brown.

If you are going on a picnic immediately, let cool slightly in the pan, then wrap in a clean kitchen towel. Otherwise, let cool completely, wrap in aluminium foil and refrigerate until required. Don't forget to take a sharp knife and platter for serving. Serve with a green salad.

In Sicily, this is known as *Cabbucio*, meaning hood or cowl, and refers to a kind of bruschetta with a lid. Authentic Italian bread is still additive-free, which means it goes stale quickly, but put yesterday's uncut loaf in a hot oven for a few minutes and it will come out like new. Cut it open while hot and anoint it with extra virgin oil and your chosen filling and you have a delicious snack. Alternatively, you can use fresh bread.

hot crusty loaf

filled with mozzarella, salami, and tomato

1 lb. round "flat" crusty Italian loaf
5 large tomatoes, thinly sliced
6½ oz. mozzarella cheese, thinly sliced
3½ sliced salami or Parma ham, or
whole anchovy fillets
a small bunch of oregano or basil
sea salt and freshly ground black pepper
extra virgin olive oil, for drizzling

serves 4

Heat the bread in a preheated oven at 425°F for 5 minutes. While the bread is still hot, cut it in half lengthways and make small incisions all over the cut surfaces of both halves of the bread. Drizzle with olive oil and sprinkle with salt, pepper, and half the oregano leaves. On the bottom half of the loaf, put a layer of tomato, followed by a layer of cheese. Top with the salami and the remaining oregano leaves. Sandwich the 2 halves together, then wrap in aluminium foil and a clean kitchen towel, and transfer it to a picnic basket. Don't forget to take a bread knife and cutting board.

Focaccia is the flat, soft springy olive oil bread from Liguria, classically topped with rosemary, olive oil, and coarse salt. In this recipe, it is rolled thinly to make it crusty. As with all bread recipes, it takes time to make and proof, so this is not a dish to make in a hurry but, if you can spare the time, it is well worth the effort. This delicious pie can be adapted for vegetarians, by omitting the cured meats and adding some other tangy ingredients such as olives, capers, or anchovies.

roasted pepper, mozzarella, and Italian cured meat focaccia pie

3 bell peppers, preferably 1 red, 1 orange, and 1 yellow, halved, deseeded and cut into 8 strips
2 garlic cloves, finely chopped
a handful of fresh parsley, finely chopped
1 14-oz. can Italian plum tomatoes, drained, deseeded, and chopped
4 oz. mozzarella cheese, thinly sliced
4 oz. dry cured meats, such as bresaola or prosciutto
1–2 teaspoons dried oregano
sea salt and freshly ground black pepper
olive oil, for frying

focaccia dough

2¼ cups "00" Italian flour or 1¼ cups all-purpose flour mixed with 1 cup cake flour
2¼ cups semolina
1 tablespoon dried yeast
2 teaspoons sea salt
5 tablespoons extra virgin olive oil, plus extra for oiling, brushing and drizzling
1⅓ cups warm water
coarse sea salt, for sprinkling

a round baking sheet, 12 inches diameter, oiled
a small blanket or a sheet of bubble wrap

serves 8–12

Heat plenty of olive oil to cover the base of a large pan, add the peppers, garlic, parsley, salt, and pepper and stir well until it starts to bubble, then reduce the heat, cover and simmer for 25 minutes or until tender. Let cool.

To make the dough, put the flours, yeast, salt, olive oil and warm water in a large mixing bowl. Work the ingredients together into a ball with your hands and then transfer to a clean floured work surface. To knead the dough, pull it into an oval shape, anchor the end nearest to you with your left fist and push the dough away from you with the base of your right fist, putting the full weight of your body behind your hand. When the dough is fully extended, roll it back up on itself and towards you with your fingers. Give the dough roll a quarter turn and repeat. Go on repeating this until the dough is smooth, soft and springy. This will take about 30 minutes. Alternatively, put the ingredients in a food processor and process for 5–10 minutes until smooth, soft and springy.

Transfer the dough to a large oiled mixing bowl, cover with plastic wrap and wrap in a blanket or in bubble wrap, then set in a warm, draft-free spot for 20 minutes, during which time the dough should double in size.

Punch down the dough for a couple of minutes to remove the air and then divide into 3 pieces. Knead the 3 pieces of dough into smooth balls. Sprinkle a clean work surface and rolling pin with plenty of flour. Set one of the dough balls in the center of the flour, then flatten it with the palm of your hand and shape it into a neat circle. Take the rolling pin and roll the pastry one way, then give it a quarter turn and roll it the other way, shaping the dough with your hands from time to time. Continue until the pastry is the same size as the baking sheet. Transfer the dough to the baking sheet and cover with the tomatoes, mozzarella, and cured meats, leaving a border of ¾ inch around the edge. Sprinkle with the oregano and drizzle with olive oil.

Roll out a second circle of dough and put this on top of the cured meats. Cover this with the peppers. Roll a third circle of dough and put this on top.

Carefully press down the edges of the pie to seal them together and prick them with a fork all the way around. Then prick the pie all over right through to the tin base. Brush the top with olive oil, sprinkle with coarse salt and cook in a preheated oven at 350°F for 45 minutes.

If you are going on a picnic immediately, wrap the focaccia and the baking sheet in a large kitchen towel and a small blanket. Otherwise, let cool, wrap in aluminium foil and refrigerate until required. Don't forget to take a bread knife and cutting board.

Two more ideas on a theme. The Rustic Loaf Filled with Ham and Apple Chutney is quintessentially British, conjuring up the memories of harvest-time picnics in the hay fields in days gone by, while the Ciabatta Bread Filled with Roasted Peppers, Jerusalem Hummus and Arugula steps straight into the 21st century, summoning up the city sandwich bar. The former can be made with hot, home-cooked ham and fresh bread, or straight from the supermarket with cold sliced ham and hot bread. The latter is a vegetarian treat that everyone will want to eat and, if you can bear it, it is well worth peeling the peppers, as it gives them a rich, fleshy texture.

rustic loaf

filled with ham and apple chutney

2¼ lb. country ham
1 bay leaf
2 8-oz. rustic loaves
2–3 tablespoons mayonnaise
2 cups shredded iceberg lettuce
2 tablespoons apple chutney

serves 4

Soak the country ham in cold water for several hours. Discard the soaking water and transfer the ham to a large pan. Fill with fresh cold water, add the bay leaf and slowly bring to the boil. Reduce the heat and simmer for 40 minutes, turning once. Let stand in the water for 20 minutes. Transfer the ham to a carving tray and thinly slice 16 oz. of the ham.

Cut one of the loaves in half lengthways and spread the halves with mayonnaise. Cover the bottom half with lettuce and half the sliced ham, then spread evenly with chutney. Sandwich the 2 halves together, then repeat with the remaining ingredients. Wrap in aluminium foil and a clean kitchen towel, then transfer to a picnic basket. Don't forget to take a bread knife and cutting board.

ciabatta

filled with roasted peppers, jerusalem hummus, and arugula

2 red bell peppers, halved and deseeded
2 yellow bell peppers, halved and deseeded
8 sprigs of rosemary
2 8-oz. ciabatta loaves
¾ cup Jerusalem Hummus (page 85) or ready-made hummus
2 large handfuls of arugula
extra virgin olive oil, for drizzling

serves 4

Put the pepper halves in a roasting pan and put a sprig of rosemary and a little olive oil inside each one. Cook in a preheated oven at 425°F for 25 minutes or until tender. Leave until cool enough to handle, then discard the rosemary and peel the pepper halves.

Put the loaves in the oven for 5 minutes to heat though. Cut in half lengthways and spread the halves with the hummus. Cover the bottom halves with arugula and the peppers, then sandwich the bread together. Wrap in aluminium foil and a clean kitchen towel, then transfer to a picnic basket. Don't forget to take a bread knife and a cutting board.

avocado, olive, and anchovy dip

Like most recipes made with avocado, the pale creamy green color of this tangy Spanish dip darkens to khaki quite quickly, so it is best made shortly before you eat it. Try burying the avocado pit in the dip, as this is supposed to prevent discoloration.

1 large avocado, peeled, pitted, and cut into chunks
4 anchovy fillets, halved
1 garlic clove, crushed
1 tablespoon ready-made olive pesto
1 tablespoon extra virgin olive oil
2 tablespoons freshly squeezed lemon juice
1 tablespoon chopped fresh parsley, plus extra to serve
a large pinch of sugar
freshly ground black pepper

serves 2–4

Put the ingredients in a food processor and reduce to a smooth dipping consistency. Transfer to a serving bowl, cover and refrigerate until required.

When ready to serve, sprinkle with parsley.

eggplant and tahini dip

This Middle Eastern meze is cool, mild and refreshing. Baked whole in a microwave or oven, the flesh of the eggplant becomes silky smooth. As well as being mixed into a dip, baked eggplant is also delicious chopped and dressed with extra virgin olive oil, seasoning and fresh herbs for a delicate appetizer or salad.

1 medium-sized eggplant, about 5 oz.
1 garlic clove, crushed
1 tablespoon freshly squeezed lemon juice
3 tablespoons extra virgin olive oil, plus extra to serve
1 tablespoon dark tahini paste
sea salt

to serve
a handful of fresh parsley, finely chopped
1 tablespoon black olives

serves 2–4

Prick the eggplant a few times with a fork and set on a piece of paper towel in a microwave oven. Cook on HIGH for 3 minutes, then turn and cook for 3 minutes more. Alternatively, bake in a preheated oven at 350°F for 20–30 minutes until soft.

Leave until cool enough to handle, then peel. Cut into 3 or 4 slices and let drain between 2 sheets of paper towel.

Transfer to a food processor with the garlic, lemon juice, olive oil, and tahini paste. Add salt to taste, then spoon into a serving dish, cover and refrigerate until required.

When ready to serve, sprinkle with parsley and olives and drizzle with olive oil.

cream cheese, walnut, and celery dip

This tasty combination is a Western classic. Try hazelnuts or blue cheese for a change.

1 package cream cheese
1 cup walnut pieces
2 tablespoons boiling water
1 tablespoon olive oil
2 tender celery ribs, finely chopped
sea salt and freshly ground black pepper

serves 2–4

Put the cheese, walnuts, water, olive oil, salt, and pepper in a food processor and reduce to a dipping consistency. Transfer to a bowl and stir in the celery. Cover and chill until required.

jerusalem hummus with toasted pine nuts

The addition of cilantro and pine nuts gives aroma and texture to hummus.

1 15-oz. can chickpeas, drained, rinsed, and dried
1 garlic clove, crushed
freshly squeezed juice of 1 lemon
2 tablespoons extra virgin olive oil
2 tablespoons dark tahini paste
½ teaspoon sea salt
3 tablespoons chopped fresh cilantro
3 tablespoons pine nuts, toasted in a dry frying pan

serves 2–4

Put the chickpeas, garlic, lemon juice, olive oil, tahini paste, salt, and ¼ cup of water in a food processor and reduce to a dipping consistency. Transfer to a bowl. Stir in most of the cilantro and pine nuts. Sprinkle with the remaining cilantro and pine nuts, then serve.

This is an eye-catching Catalan salad that I discovered in Barcelona. The hard-cooked eggs looked stunning placed in neat lines on top of the lentils. Each one was artfully dressed with a swirl of anchovy, short chive plumes and small mint leaves, giving them the appearance of tiny wedding hats. As this would be difficult to transport on a picnic, you may prefer to simply stir the herbs into the lentils and scatter the eggs and anchovies on top. Meat eaters may like to boil the lentils in water previously used for cooking ham, as it gives them extra depth of flavor.

herbed lentil salad

with hard-cooked eggs and anchovies

2 cups dried French lentils
1 garlic clove, very thinly sliced
a handful of fresh mint, plus extra to serve
a handful of fresh cilantro or parsley, plus extra to serve
a handful of fresh chives, finely snipped
4 hard-cooked eggs, chopped
8 anchovy fillets
olive oil, for frying

dressing
1 tablespoon red wine vinegar
3 tablespoons extra virgin olive oil
1 teaspoon mustard powder
1 teaspoon sugar
sea salt and freshly ground black pepper

serves 4

Cook the lentils in boiling water for 25 minutes, then drain. Cover the base of a large saucepan with olive oil, add the garlic and heat gently. When the garlic starts to color, discard it. Add the lentils and toss until well coated, then let cool a little.

To make the dressing, put the vinegar, olive oil, mustard powder, sugar, salt, and pepper in a screw-top jar. Seal and shake well.

Chop the mint and cilantro together finely, then add to the lentils with the chives and dressing and mix well. Transfer to a plastic container with a lid, then crumble the egg on top and scatter over the anchovies. Sprinkle with mint and cilantro before serving.

Variation Use boiled rice or couscous rather than lentils.

This pretty chicken dish (my take on Coronation Chicken) makes a delicious centerpiece for a special picnic, summer buffet, or family meal. The cool fruit contrasts with the creamy texture of the chicken and the spice cuts the rich mayonnaise, making a refreshing dish that can be dressed up or down according to the occasion. Your own freshly roasted or poached chicken will absorb the flavors better than one that has been left to go completely cold. However, you can make a swift version using a ready-cooked chicken and curry powder.

spiced chicken and mango mayonnaise with pistachios

1 lb. freshly cooked chicken meat, cut into strips
1 small ripe mango, peeled, pitted, and cut into ½-inch cubes
1 large slice of ripe melon, peeled, deseeded and cut into ½-inch cubes
1 cup seedless grapes, halved
2 tablespoons finely chopped celery
¾ cup mayonnaise
freshly squeezed juice of ½ lemon, plus 1 tablespoon to serve
½ teaspoon mixed mustard seeds
½ teaspoon cumin seeds
½ teaspoon coriander seeds
2 teaspoons ground turmeric
¼ teaspoon ground red pepper
1 teaspoon ground ginger
2 tablespoons shelled pistachios
sea salt and freshly ground black pepper, plus 1 tablespoon to serve

to serve

2 large handfuls mixed salad leaves, such as mâche, baby spinach, or radicchio
1 lemon, thinly sliced (optional)
1 tablespoon chopped fresh cilantro

serves 4–6

Put the strips of chicken in a large bowl with the mango, melon, grapes, and celery. Add the mayonnaise and lemon juice and mix well. Put the mustard seeds, cumin seeds, and coriander seeds in a mortar and grind finely with a pestle. Add to the chicken with the turmeric, ground red pepper, ginger, 1 tablespoon of the pistachios, ½ teaspoon salt, and some black pepper. Mix well, cover and chill until required.

When ready to serve, arrange the salad leaves around the edge of a serving dish, drizzle with the lemon juice, add salt and pepper and top with lemon slices, if using. Spoon the chicken salad into the middle of the dish and sprinkle with the cilantro and the remaining pistachios. Cover closely with plastic wrap until ready to serve.

A fresh-tasting tabbouleh salad is a welcome dish on any summer table. In the Lebanon, where it originated, it is served as a starter with hummus and other meze, and it is also popular for Sunday picnics. This recipe is based on an authentic tabbouleh recipe, but I have added gherkins and horseradish sauce to complement the pastrami. I have also added cherry tomatoes instead of the chopped whole ones traditionally used.

cherry tomato tabbouleh salad

with pastrami

1 cup bulgur wheat
2 handfuls of fresh parsley
a handful of fresh mint
a handful of fresh basil
a small bunch of scallions, finely chopped
1 garlic clove, finely chopped
1 tablespoon cocktail gherkins
1 pint firm cherry tomatoes, halved
6 tablespoons olive oil
2 tablespoons freshly squeezed lemon juice
1 tablespoon horseradish (optional)
12 slices of pastrami, about 6 oz., to serve
sea salt and freshly ground black pepper

serves 4–6

Put the bulgur wheat in a large bowl, add enough cold water to cover and let stand for 30 minutes. Drain if necessary, pat dry on a clean kitchen towel and transfer to a large bowl. Chop the parsley, mint, and basil together and add to the bulgur wheat. Add the scallions, garlic, gherkins, tomatoes, olive oil, lemon juice, horseradish, if using, and salt and pepper to taste. Cover and let stand for a couple of hours to allow the flavors to develop.

When ready to serve, arrange the pastrami around the edge of a serving dish and pile the tabbouleh in the middle of the dish. Cover closely with plastic wrap until ready to serve.

Variation Serve with smoked fish, broken into pieces or cubed feta or tofu instead of pastrami, if you prefer.

I love homemade cake and the plainer, the better. I have never seen the need for sickly fillings and toppings that mask the flavor. At most, all a good cake needs is a simple frosting, melted chocolate topping or jam in the middle. This freshly baked, moist yet crumbly aromatic pineapple loaf needs no more than a dusting of confectioners' sugar on top. When taking a cake on a picnic, don't forget to put a knife in the tin.

pineapple and thyme loaf cake

10 tablespoons unsalted butter or margarine
¾ cup granulated sugar
3 beaten eggs
½ cup self-rising flour
½ cup semolina
2 teaspoons baking powder
8-oz. can pineapple chunks, chopped in a food processor
1 tablespoon finely chopped fresh thyme
1 tablespoon vanilla sugar or 1 teaspoon pure vanilla extract
confectioners' sugar, to dust (optional)

9 x 5 x 3-inch loaf pan, lined with wax paper

serves 8

Put the butter and sugar in a large mixing bowl and beat until light and fluffy. Add the eggs a little at a time, beating well after each addition; it may be necessary to add a little of the flour to prevent the mixture curdling. Fold in the remaining flour, semolina, baking powder, pineapple, thyme, and vanilla sugar.

Bake in a preheated oven at 375°F for 30 minutes or until well risen and golden. When the cake is cool enough to handle, turn out onto a cooling rack and let cool. Dust with confectioners' sugar, then wrap in aluminium foil and transfer to a tin.

Children of all ages love chocolate muffins and the more chocolaty, the better, so I have added chocolate spread to this recipe to give them extra kid appeal. What better way of getting them to cook than asking them to help you make their favorite treat? Not that it is ever a problem when cake is on the menu—it's keeping their fingers out of the mixing bowl and the mixture off their faces that is the problem. This recipe is so simple to make that older children can make them by themselves.

triple chocolate chip muffins

1⅔ cups self-rising flour
2 teaspoons baking powder
2 tablespoons cocoa powder
1 cup granulated sugar
3½ oz. good-quality bittersweet chocolate, chopped
1 egg, beaten
¼ cup chocolate and hazelnut spread
6 tablespoons vegetable oil
⅔ cup milk

12 paper muffin cases
a 12-hole muffin pan

makes 12

Set the paper muffin cases in the pan. Sift the flour, baking powder, and cocoa powder into a mixing bowl, then add the sugar, chocolate, egg, chocolate and hazelnut spread, and vegetable oil and mix well with a wooden spoon. Add the milk a little at a time, stirring well between each addition, until the mixture has a good pouring consistency.

Ladle the mixture into the lined pan and bake in a preheated oven at 400°F for 20–25 minutes or until the muffins are well risen and firm to the touch. Transfer to a cooling rack, let cool and transfer to a tin until required.

Variation Substitute the chocolate and hazlenut spread with ¼ cup of freshly made espresso coffee and the chocolate with 1 cup chopped walnuts. Add an extra ¼ cup of sugar and an extra egg to the mixture.

traditional english apple tart

Of all the fancy desserts there are, there is nothing to beat a simple baked apple tart. It's quick and simple to make, delicious and it lends itself perfectly to the picnic basket, hot or cold. Slivers of cheddar cheese go well with it too. Interestingly, it was one of the few English things that I was asked to make when I lived in Italy. Children love small apple pies, which can be made in jam tart tins, but you need to stew the apple to a mush and let it cool before using.

2¼ cups all-purpose flour
a pinch of sea salt
10 tablespoons chilled butter, diced
5 tablespoons chilled water
2¼ lb. cooking apples, peeled, cored, and thinly sliced
½ cup granulated sugar, plus extra to decorate and to serve
cream or yogurt, to serve

a shallow pie dish, about 10 inches diameter, greased

serves 6

Put the flour, salt and butter in a large mixing bowl and rub in the butter with your fingertips until the mixture resembles fine breadcrumbs. Add the water and work the mixture together to form a dough. This should be done quickly and lightly with your fingertips or the blade of a round-bladed knife. Alternatively, put the ingredients in a food processor and process until the ingredients are reduced to a dough.

Divide the dough in half and work each half into a neat ball. Sprinkle a clean work surface and a rolling pin with plenty of flour. Set 1 of the pastry balls in the center of the flour, flatten it with the palm of your hand and shape into a neat circle. Roll the pastry one way, then give it a quarter turn and roll it the other way, shaping the dough back into a circle from time to time. Continue until the pastry is slightly larger than the pie dish.

Roll the pastry around the rolling pin and transfer it carefully to the pie dish, open it out and smooth it to line the dish and the border. Fill with the apple slices, then brush the border with water. Roll out the second ball of dough as before and put this on top of the apples. Trim off the excess pastry with a sharp knife. Press down the border with your thumb to seal it, creating a regular pattern around the edge as you do so. Brush the top of the pie with water and sprinkle with sugar.

Set the pie on a baking sheet in the center of the preheated oven and bake at 425°F for 20 minutes, then reduce the heat to 300°F and bake for 20 minutes more. Check to see if the fruit is cooked by gently pushing a skewer into it. If it offers resistance, it is not cooked, so cook for a further 10 minutes. If you are going on a picnic immediately, allow to cool a little, wrap in a clean kitchen towel and a small blanket and don't forget a pie server. Serve warm or cold with sugar and cream.

elegant al fresco

Whether it is a long leisurely lunch in the shade, a romantic dinner for two, or a supper party with friends under the stars, dining outdoors should be every bit as luxurious as a dinner party indoors and will prove more memorable. There is an abundance of fresh produce available in the summer to inspire colorful appetizers and side dishes, simple meat, fish, pasta, and rice dishes, and last but not least luscious, indulgent fruity puddings.

This three-in-one appetizer is substantial enough to serve as a light lunch. It consists of peppers stuffed with mozzarella and anchovy or prosciutto, and mushrooms stuffed with crabmeat, both topped with herbed breadcrumbs and tomatoes with herbed breadcrumbs. The inspiration came from a simple herbed tomato recipe, *pomodori raganati*, that I picked up in Liguria, which goes well on its own or with meat and fish dishes.

trio of stuffed vegetables

2 large tomatoes, halved and deseeded
a handful of fresh parsley
a handful of fresh mint
a handful of fresh basil
1 cup soft white breadcrumbs (page 54)
4 garlic cloves, crushed
2 yellow peppers, halved and deseeded, stems retained
2 medium or large flat mushrooms, stems discarded
8 anchovy fillets, chopped, or 1 slice of prosciutto, cut into quarters
3 oz. mozzarella cheese, cut into 4 slices
4 oz. crabmeat
1 tablespoon mayonnaise
a pinch of ground red pepper
2 teaspoons freshly squeezed lemon juice
sea salt and freshly ground black pepper
extra virgin olive oil, for oiling and drizzling
arugula, to serve

serves 4

Invert the tomato halves onto a paper towel and let drain.

Put the herbs, breadcrumbs, and garlic in a food processor and finely chop, then add plenty of salt and pepper.

Arrange the cut pepper halves and mushrooms in an oiled roasting pan, cut side up, and season with salt and pepper and a few drops of olive oil.

Divide the anchovies between the pepper halves, put a slice of mozzarella on top and cover with one-third of the breadcrumbs.

Put the crabmeat, mayonnaise, ground red pepper, and lemon juice in a bowl and mix well. Spoon the crabmeat mixture on top of the mushrooms and cover with one-third of the breadcrumbs.

Dry the tomato halves carefully with paper towels, then add to the roasting pan. Season with salt and pepper, drizzle with a little olive oil, then cover with one-third of the breadcrumbs. Scatter any remaining breadcrumbs around the vegetables.

Drizzle olive oil over all the vegetables and bake in a preheated oven at 425 ºF for 20 minutes or until the vegetables are tender and the breadcrumbs crisp on top. Serve with arugula.

Chilled soups are a summer delight that had to be included here. I hovered between two of my favorites, watercress and asparagus, both refreshing in taste and intense in colour, until I saw this combination of flavorsome salad leaves. I was sure they would make a cracking summer soup and they do! Plunging lightly cooked leaves and vegetables into ice water helps preserve their natural fresh green pigment.

chilled spinach, arugula, and watercress soup

4 shallots, chopped
2 garlic cloves, chopped
½ nutmeg, grated, plus extra to serve
⅓ cup white wine
1¾ cups vegetable stock
8 oz. mixed spinach, arugula, and watercress leaves
¾ cup cream or yogurt
sea salt and freshly ground black pepper
olive oil, for frying

to serve
4 teaspoons cream
4 large leaves of arugula

serves 4

Heat enough olive oil to cover the base of a frying pan, add the shallots, garlic, and nutmeg and fry over low heat until the onions are soft. Add the wine and stock and bring to the boil, then simmer for 10 minutes. Remove from the heat and let cool.

Put the spinach, arugula, and watercress in a large pan containing 1 quart of lightly salted boiling water, gently submerse the leaves with a spoon and blanch for 60 seconds. Drain and plunge the leaves into a bowl of cold water and ice to chill quickly. Drain and squeeze out the excess water with your hands.

Put the leaves and the soup in a food processor and blend to a smooth consistency. Add the cream and season with salt and pepper to taste. Cover and chill for at least 2 hours or overnight.

Ladle the soup into bowls, feather with cream and serve with arugula leaves and grated nutmeg.

Cichetti are the Venetian answer to tapas. They are served as snacks in all the bars around Venice and go down well at lunchtime with a glass of Prosecco, the local sparkling wine, as you watch the world flood by. Speck is a cured ham, similar to prosciutto, made in the Alto Adige region to the north of the Veneto.

speck and crayfish cichetti

laced with chile

¼ cup mayonnaise
2 teaspoons sun-dried tomato paste
a pinch ground red pepper, plus extra to serve
1 teaspoon freshly squeezed lime juice
finely pared zest of 1 unwaxed lime
1 celery rib, finely chopped
3 oz. cooked crayfish tails or shrimp, shelled
3 thin slices of whole-wheat bread
3 oz. thinly sliced speck or prosciutto
4 small tender lettuce leaves, to serve
butter, for spreading

serves 4

Put the mayonnaise, sun-dried tomato paste, ground red pepper and lime juice in a bowl with 1 teaspoon of the lime zest, then stir. Add the celery and crayfish tails and mix well, then cover and leave until required.

When ready to serve, butter the bread slices, trim the crusts and cut each slice into 4 squares.

Using scissors, cut the speck into 12 pieces. Put them on the bread, then spoon the crayfish mixture on top. Scatter over a couple of strands of lime zest and sprinkle with ground red pepper. Serve with lettuce leaves.

The combination of monkfish and scallops on a kabob is delicious. They both have solid textures and distinctive flavors. The addition of thinly sliced salami or pancetta adds a crisp saltiness. By cooking kabobs on a baking sheet in the oven rather than under a broiler, they do not dry out and the breadcrumbs soak up the juices that would otherwise be lost. Prepare the skewers in advance and cook them at the last minute.

spiked monkfish, scallops, and cherry tomatoes in crispy breadcrumbs

2 tablespoons all-purpose flour
16–18 oz. monkfish or other thick white fish, cut into 12 square chunks
8 small or 4 large raw, shelled scallops, 5–7 oz., halved
2½ oz. thinly sliced Milano salami or pancetta, cut into strips
12 cherry tomatoes
2 tablespoons extra virgin olive oil, plus extra for drizzling
¼ cup soft white breadcrumbs (page 54)
sea salt and freshly ground black pepper

to serve
balsamic vinegar
Lemon Roast Potato Wedges (page 121; optional)
arugula and romaine lettuce salad

4 metal skewers

serves 4

Put the flour in a large bowl and season with salt and pepper. Add the fish chunks and scallops and shake the bowl until they are well coated with flour.

Wrap the monkfish in the salami strips. Thread the monkfish pieces, scallops, and tomatoes onto the skewers, starting and finishing with a tomato.

Oil the base of a rectangular roasting tin with the olive oil. Roll the kabobs in the oil one at a time, then arrange them in the roasting tin. Sprinkle the breadcrumbs on and around the kebabs and then drizzle with more olive oil.

Cook in a preheated oven at 220°C (425°F) Gas 7 for 10 minutes or until the fish is set and the breadcrumbs golden. Remove the roasting tin from the oven and drizzle balsamic vinegar over the kabobs. Serve with lemon roast potato wedges, if liked, and an arugula and romaine lettuce salad.

Salmon is a great summer standby and not in any way the luxury it once was. A whole cooked salmon makes a magnificent centerpiece for a summer party, but take care not to overcook it. The general rule of cooking fish applies—undercook it and let stand for a few minutes and it will finish cooking in its own heat without drying out. This rich tangy topping can be prepared well in advance and the salmon can be cooked at the last minute. This crumble can also be served cold.

salmon, mascarpone, caper, and sun-dried tomato crumble

2 tablespoons salted capers, rinsed and dried*
1 oz. soft sun-dried tomatoes
a large handful of fresh parsley
¾ cup mascarpone cheese
⅓ cup all-purpose flour
1½ tablespoons butter
finely chopped zest and freshly squeezed juice of ½ unwaxed lemon
4 salmon fillets, about 1 lb.
sea salt and freshly ground black pepper
extra virgin olive oil, for oiling

to serve
lemon wedges
thin green beans (haricots verts)
boiled new potatoes tossed in olive oil and chopped fresh mint (optional)

serves 4

Put the capers, sun-dried tomatoes, and parsley on a cutting board and chop together finely. Put the mascarpone cheese in a bowl and add the chopped caper mixture.

Put the flour and the butter in a bowl and rub in the butter with your fingertips until the mixture resembles fine breadcrumbs. Add salt and pepper and stir in the lemon zest. Cover and refrigerate until required.

Arrange the salmon pieces in an oiled roasting pan, season with salt and pepper and drizzle with the lemon juice. Spread the mascarpone cheese mixture on the top of the salmon and sprinkle with the crumble. Cook in a preheated oven at 425°F for 10 minutes until the salmon is just set and the crumble is crisp and golden. Transfer to a serving plate and serve with lemon wedges, beans, and new potatoes tossed in olive oil and mint, if liked.

***Note** You can use capers in brine rather than salted capers, but you will need to add a pinch of salt to the mascarpone cheese mixture.

Variation To prepare a whole side of salmon, line a long roasting pan with baking parchment, place the salmon on top and proceed as above. Cook for 20–30 minutes until golden on top, then let rest for 10 minutes before serving.

This quick version of *spaghetti ai frutti di mare* is a great recipe for a summer dinner party. The tomato sauce can be made in advance, the spaghetti cooked at the last minute, the seafood added and then everything put together and served. Make sure you use fine spaghettini rather than the thicker spaghetti, as it cooks more quickly and you'll be surprised at the difference it makes to the lightness of the dish. I always stock up on good dried Italian pasta whenever I see it, which generally means on a visit to an Italian store. The sauce would also work well in a risotto.

instant seafood spaghetti

2 14-oz cans Italian plum tomatoes, drained and deseeded, juice reserved
5 tablespoons extra virgin olive oil, plus extra to serve
4 garlic cloves, chopped
1 small piece of fresh chile, to taste
3½ oz. mixed, cooked seafood, such as squid rings, shrimp, mussels, or clams
2 tablespoons finely chopped fresh flat leaf parsley, plus extra to serve
16 oz. spaghettini
sea salt and freshly ground black pepper

serves 4

Put the tomatoes, olive oil, garlic, and chile in a heavy-based saucepan, cover and simmer over low heat for 30 minutes or until the tomatoes are reduced to a creamy mass. Stir from time to time to ensure the sauce does not stick to the bottom of the pan. Add a little of the reserved tomato juice to keep the sauce moist, if necessary. Discard the chile and reduce the sauce to a smooth pulp using a potato masher.

Add the seafood, parsley, and plenty of black pepper to the saucepan and simmer very gently. Meanwhile, cook the spaghettini in plenty of salted boiling water, following the instructions on the packet, until al dente. Drain immediately, reserving 2 tablespoons of the cooking water, and return to the cooking pan.

Add the sauce and the reserved cooking water to the pasta pan and mix until the sauce is well distributed. Transfer to a serving dish, sprinkle with parsley and black pepper and drizzle with olive oil. Serve immediately.

Variation Add 2 drained cans of clams or tuna fish to the tomato sauce instead of the mixed seafood.

This delicious combination of chicken and caramelized peaches originated in Iran and the addition of pistachios fits in with its Middle Eastern origins. Shelled pistachios are prepared for use in confectionery and are generally sold in Middle Eastern stores. They are fantastic for use in all kinds of dishes because the skin is removed, revealing that distinctive pistachio green. This dish can be prepared in advance and simply reheated when required, adding the extra fruit and nuts just before serving.

spiced chicken

with pistachios and caramelized peaches

8 chicken thighs, skin on
½ cup chicken stock
1 onion, finely chopped
2 tablespoons ground turmeric
2 teaspoons ground cinnamon
2 tablespoons grappa or vodka
3 peaches or kiwi fruit, peeled, pitted and quartered
freshly squeezed juice of 1 lime or lemon
1 tablespoon brown sugar
1 tablespoon chopped or pistachios, plus extra to serve
sea salt and freshly ground black pepper
olive oil, for frying

to serve

1 peach or 2 kiwi fruit, peeled, pitted, and sliced (optional)
boiled rice

serves 4

Rub the chicken pieces with plenty of salt and pepper. Heat enough oil to cover the base of a large frying pan and fry the chicken pieces over high heat until golden on all sides. Transfer to a plate.

Pour off the excess fat from the frying pan and reserve. Add the stock to the pan and set it over low heat to deglaze, then scrape up the juices and reserve. Return 2 tablespoons of chicken fat to the pan and add the onion, turmeric, and cinnamon, mix well and cook over low heat until the onion is soft.

Increase the heat and return the chicken to the pan. Turn once or twice in the onion mixture, add the grappa and continue to cook until it has evaporated. Pour the stock back into the pan, cover and cook for 20 minutes. Turn the chicken and simmer again for 20 minutes.

Heat 1 tablespoon of olive oil over low heat, then add the peaches and cook for 1 minute. Add the lime juice and sugar and simmer for 1 minute. Add the pistachios, stir gently, then cover and cook for 20 minutes.

Transfer to a serving dish and scatter over extra pistachios and peach slices, if using. Serve with boiled rice.

Roast guinea fowl is a treat; half chicken, half game, it is full of flavor. Where we might roast whole birds and quite large pieces, Italians tend to cut poultry and meat into small pieces that roast very quickly and absorb other ingredients more directly, giving great finger-licking potential. This recipe makes for a quick, easy and exotic roast to serve for a special meal. Adding the ready-boiled potatoes and beans to the meat in the cooking pan and mixing them up means that none of the meat juices will be wasted.

italian roast guinea fowl
with new potatoes and green beans

3 lb. guinea fowl
2 tablespoons butter
1½ lb. new potatoes
6 oz. green beans
½ cup vegetable stock
sea salt
Radicchio Plumes (page 121), to serve

serves 4–6

If using a whole guinea fowl, cut them in half lengthways, then cut each half into 6 evenly sized pieces.

Arrange the guinea fowl in a large roasting tin, dot with butter, and sprinkle generously with salt. Cover with aluminium foil and let stand at room temperature for 1 hour. Remove the foil, put the pan in the middle of a preheated oven and roast at 400°F for 30 minutes or until golden brown and tender, turning the guinea fowl at least once.

Meanwhile, put the potatoes in a small saucepan of salted water and boil until tender, then drain. Cook the beans in the same way for about 8 minutes until al dente, then drain.

Add the potatoes and beans to the roasting dish and stir well to coat with the pan juices. Transfer the meat and vegetables to a serving plate.

Deglaze the tin with the stock, boil until reduced by half, then pour over the meat and vegetables. Serve with radicchio plumes.

Variation Free-range chicken or rabbit are also good cooked in this simple, quick and delicious way.

Steak is everybody's favorite, but beware, as it can sometimes be tough. Fillet steak is always reliable, but other steaks, however good in flavor, can vary. I find freezing steak for a few days prior to use helps. The art of cooking a good steak is to have the pan very hot before you put the meat in and to add the oil or butter at the same time as the meat. This way, the minute the meat makes contact with the pan, it will sear the outside, capturing all the juices inside.

fanned steak

with arugula crème fraîche

2 tablespoons olive oil, plus extra to serve
4 tenderloin steaks, about 1½ lb., or 4 rump steaks, about 1½ lb.
1 garlic clove, unpeeled and halved
sea salt and freshly ground black pepper

arugula crème fraîche
a large handful of arugula
1 teaspoon mixed mustard seeds, crushed
2 garlic cloves, cut into 3 pieces
⅔ cup crème fraîche or sour cream
sea salt and freshly ground black pepper

to serve
Lemon Roast Potato Wedges (page 121)
cherry tomatoes
arugula leaves

serves 4

To make the arugula crème fraîche, put the arugula, mustard seeds, and garlic in a food processor and chop finely. Put the crème fraîche in a mixing bowl and stir in the arugula mixture. Add ½ teaspoon salt and pepper to taste.

Put a large frying pan over medium heat. When the pan is hot, increase the heat and add the olive oil and the steak at the same time. Sear quickly on both sides until dark brown for rare steak. For medium or well-done steak, reduce the heat to medium and cook for a further 2–6 minutes, according to taste.

Transfer the steaks to a cutting board and rub both sides of the meat with the cut garlic and sprinkle with salt. Cut the steak diagonally into 5 or 6 slices.

Arrange a fan of sliced steak on each plate and sprinkle with black pepper and drizzle with olive oil. Serve immediately with the arugula crème fraîche, lemon roast potato wedges, cherry tomatoes, and arugula leaves.

Variation Serve the steak on char-grilled ciabatta bread spread with the arugula fraîche, topped with a tomato and some arugula.

Made with almonds, basil, and tomato, this pesto recipe comes from Trapane in Sicily, where it is known as *pesto trapanese*. It is traditionally served with a regional pasta called *busiate*, which is similar to *bucatini*. The rich smoky flavor of toasted almonds and the peppery flavor of the basil permeate the risotto rice, making the perfect combination. It is highly recommended for non-vegetarians as well.

risotto with sicilian pesto

2 shallots, finely chopped
1 lb. risotto rice, preferably vialone nano
⅓ cup white wine
1 quart hot vegetable stock
extra virgin olive oil, for frying, plus extra to serve

sicilian pesto
½ cup toasted sliced almonds
2 large handfuls fresh basil leaves
4 garlic cloves, lightly crushed
2 28-oz cans Italian plum tomatoes drained, deseeded, and chopped
½ cup olive oil
1½ cups freshly grated pecorino cheese
sea salt and freshly ground black pepper

to serve
toasted sliced almonds
freshly grated pecorino cheese

serves 4

To make the pesto, put the almonds in a food processor with a pinch of salt and grind finely. Transfer to a large bowl.

Put the basil, garlic, and tomato in a food processor and reduce to a paste. Add to the ground almonds and stir in the olive oil, pecorino cheese, and a good grinding of salt and pepper to taste. Mix well and let rest for at least 2 hours.

Cover the base of a large, heavy-based pan with olive oil, heat gently and add the shallots and 2 tablespoons of water. Cook until the shallots are transparent. Add the rice, increase the heat and cook for 2 minutes, stirring continuously. Add the wine and let it evaporate, then reduce the heat.

Level the rice and carefully spoon 10 ladles of freshly boiled stock over the rice, cover with a lid and cook on low heat for 15 minutes. After this time, add the pesto and mix energetically for 1 minute. Turn off the heat, cover and let stand for 4–5 minutes.

Transfer the risotto to a serving dish or individual plates, then drizzle with olive oil and sprinkle with almond slices. Serve immediately with pecorino cheese.

Note If ready-toasted sliced almonds are not available, put untoasted sliced almonds on a heavy baking sheet and bake in a preheated oven at 200°F for 40 minutes or until golden brown. Remove the almonds from the sheet and let cool before grinding.

I love vegetables of every kind, not least of all because they come and go with the seasons. Summer vegetables, such as new potatoes, young carrots, peas, runner beans, and fava beans, need little more than rapid cooking in salted water, with perhaps the addition of a little butter or olive oil, black pepper, and a few chopped herbs. However, if you are just going to serve one single vegetable to accompany a meal, here are some simple ways of enhancing them.

green beans
with tomato and garlic

8 oz. thin green beans (haricots verts), trimmed
1 tablespoon extra virgin olive oil
1 garlic clove, finely chopped
2 whole canned plum tomatoes, drained, deseeded, and chopped
sea salt and freshly ground black pepper

serves 4

Boil the beans in a saucepan of lightly salted water until cooked al dente, then drain. Heat the olive oil in a small saucepan over medium heat, add the garlic and tomato and cook until it starts to sizzle. Add the beans, reduce the heat and continue to cook for 5 minutes, stirring from time to time. Add salt and pepper to taste. Serve hot or cold.

Variation Try cooking broccoli, asparagus, and fava beans this way.

lemon roast potato wedges

4 medium potatoes, cut into 8 wedges each
freshly squeezed juice of ½ lemon
1–2 tablespoons extra virgin olive oil
sea salt and freshly ground black pepper

serves 4

Put the potato wedges in a roasting pan, add the lemon juice and season with salt, and pepper. Drizzle with the olive oil and stir well. Cook in a preheated oven at 425ºF for 20–30 minutes until crisp and golden, turning once or twice. Transfer to a serving dish and serve.

Variation When the potatoes are ready, add 1 pint cherry tomatoes pricked with the point of a knife, then stir into the potatoes and return to the oven for 5 minutes or until the tomato skins start to split.

radicchio plumes

2 heads of radicchio or endive, quartered
2 tablespoons extra virgin olive oil, plus extra to serve
sea salt and freshly ground black pepper

a ridged stovetop grill pan

serves 4

Arrange the radicchio quarters, cut side up, on a plate. Dress with the olive oil and season with salt and pepper. Cover with plastic wrap and set aside for at least 1 hour.

Heat a ridged stovetop grill pan over medium heat for 10 minutes until very hot. Arrange the radicchio diagonally across the pan. Turn the pieces with tongs from time to time until striped with grill marks on all sides. Transfer to a serving plate, drizzle with olive oil and serve.

Pannacotta, which literally means "cooked cream", comes from Italy and in its classic form is flavored with vanilla. Italian Galliano, the key ingredient in a Harvey Wallbanger cocktail, is a golden, vanilla-flavored liqueur. The creamy just-set texture of the pannacotta with summer fruits makes a pleasing change from the usual cream or custard.

pannacotta galliano

with summer fruit compote

¾ cup heavy cream
¾ cup, plus 2 tablespoons milk
2 tablespoons boiling water
⅓ cup granulated sugar
2 tablespoons Galliano liqueur or 1 teaspoon pure vanilla extract
1 tablespoon powdered gelatine

summer fruit compote

1½ cups blueberries (optional)
¼–⅓ cup granulated sugar
1 cup raspberries or loganberries
1 cup small strawberries

4 ramekins

serves 4

Put the cream and milk in a small saucepan, simmer gently for 5 minutes over low heat, then add the sugar and the Galliano.

Pour the boiling water into a small heatproof dish and sprinkle the gelatine over the surface (make sure that the tablespoon is level). Let stand for a few seconds until the gelatine absorbs the water. Stir until the gelatine has dissolved, then add it to the cream mixture, stirring well. Pour the cream mixture through a sieve into a jug, pushing any bits through the sieve with the back of a wooden spoon. Pour the mixture into 4 ramekins and chill overnight or until set.

To make the summer fruit compote, put the blueberries in a saucepan, if using, with ¼ cup of the sugar and 2 tablespoons of water. Set over low heat and cook until the juices start to run. Add the raspberries and strawberries, stir carefully, switch off the heat and let cool. Taste and add extra sugar, if necessary, then cover and chill until required.

When ready to serve, dip the ramekins of pannacotta quickly in shallow boiling water, then invert onto 4 serving plates. Holding the plate and ramekin together, give it a firm shake, then turn out the pannacotta carefully onto each plate. It should be quite wobbly and will plop out of the ramekin onto the plate. Add a spoonful of compote, then serve.

Variation Serve the pannacotta with shavings of dark chocolate instead of fruit.

nectarines in Sambuca and lime juice

Sambuca is a sweet Italian liqueur made from elderflowers popularized when Italian restaurants took to serving it with a burning coffee bean floating on the top. Its flowery makeup is suited to summer fruits and, if you are lucky enough to live in an area where elder grows, you can strew the delicate little summer flowers over the fruit just before serving.

8 ripe nectarines
3 tablespoons granulated sugar
2 tablespoons Sambuca
finely grated zest and freshly squeezed juice of 1 unwaxed lime
lime wedges, to serve

serves 4

Slice the nectarines thinly, discarding the pit and put in a bowl. Add the sugar, Sambuca, and lime juice, cover and leave for a couple of hours to marinate, if possible. When ready to serve, transfer to serving bowls, then sprinkle with the lime zest and serve with lime wedges.

pineapple, mango, avocado, and banana

with white rum and mint

Avocados tend to be served in savory salads and appetizers, but in fact their creamy texture and delicate flavor is delicious in fruit salads too. This tropical combination with white rum and mint creates a refreshing and eye-catching close to an *al fresco* summer meal.

1 pineapple, peeled, cored and cut into cubes
1 mango, peeled, pitted and cut into cubes
a handful of fresh mint leaves, plus extra sprigs to serve
2 tablespoons white rum
¼ cup sugar
1 banana
1 avocado

serves 4

Put the pineapple and mango in a bowl, add the mint, rum, and sugar and mix well, then cover and chill until required.

When ready to serve, peel and slice the banana, and peel, pit and cut the avocado into cubes. Add to the pineapple and mango and stir well. Serve topped with mint sprigs.

Note If you like, you can serve the fruit in the pineapple shell. Choose a pineapple with fresh green leaves and quarter it lengthways. Take care not to puncture the shell when you remove the flesh, then wrap the pineapple shells in plastic wrap and put in the refrigerator until ready to serve.

Frangipane tart is one of those classic recipes that turn a seasonal summer fruit into a luxurious treat. The combination of crisp short pastry, fluffy almond sponge cake and the tart flavors of summer fruits is a delight. Although it is not difficult to make, it does need time devoted to it, but the end result is well worth the effort.

blueberry frangipane tart

1½ cups blueberries, plums, or rhubarb
2 tablespoons sugar
confectioners' sugar, to serve

pastry
⅔ cup plus 1 tablespoon flour
1 tablespoon cornstarch
3 tablespoons confectioners' sugar
a pinch of salt
4 tablespoons butter, softened
1 small egg yolk
1 tablespoon dry vermouth or ice water

frangipane
½ cup granulated sugar
6 tablespoons butter, softened
2 eggs, lightly beaten
2 tablespoons cornstarch
2 teaspoons baking powder
⅔ cup ground almonds

a loose-bottomed tart pan or a pie dish, 9–10 inch diameter, greased

serves 6

To make the pastry, put the ingredients in a bowl and work them quickly and lightly into a smooth ball with your hands. Wrap in plastic wrap and chill in the refrigerator for 1 hour.

To make the frangipane, put the sugar and butter in a bowl and beat until light and creamy. Add the eggs a little at a time, beating well as you do so. Add the cornstarch, baking powder, and almonds, then gently fold into the mixture.

Sprinkle a clean work surface and rolling pin with plenty of flour. Set the pastry in the center of the flour, then flatten it with the palm of your hand and shape it into a neat circle. Take the rolling pin and roll the pastry one way, then give it a quarter turn and roll it the other way, shaping the dough back into a circle with your hands from time to time. Continue until the pastry is slighty larger than the pan. Roll the pastry loosely around the rolling pin and transfer it carefully to the greased pan, pressing the pastry carefully into the sides. Trim any overlapping pastry and prick the base with a fork.

Add the blueberries, sprinkle with the sugar, then spoon the frangipane over the top, taking care to seal the fruit completely underneath.

Transfer to a preheated oven and bake at 350ºF for 45 minutes or until the frangipane is well risen, golden and springy to the touch. After 25 minutes, open the oven door carefully so as not to allow too much heat to escape and, if the tart is getting too brown, lower the heat to 325°F for the final 20 minutes. Serve hot or cold dusted with confectioners' sugar.

Variation Try using apricots, peaches, rhubarb, or plums, depending on the season.

Tiramisù **is Italian for pick-me-up and this recipe is my summer adaptation of the popular Italian dessert of that name. The original—created in Treviso in the Veneto more years ago than I care to remember—is flavored with espresso coffee, but it lends itself very well to other flavors, especially fruit, and I have developed several versions according to season.**

rhubarb pick-me-up

1 lb. rhubarb, chopped
¾ cup granulated sugar
½ teaspoon ground aniseed, plus extra to serve
6 large egg yolks
1 cup mascarpone cheese
1 tablespoon grappa or other white liqueur
2 egg whites
24 ladyfingers

to serve
confectioners' sugar
3 whole star anise pods

serves 8

Put the rhubarb in a saucepan with ½ cup water. Bring to the boil, then add ½ cup of the sugar and simmer for about 10 minutes until soft.

Put the rhubarb in a dish and add the aniseed. Stir well, then drain thoroughly and reserve the juice in a large, shallow container.

Put the egg yolks and the remaining sugar in a large bowl and whisk until thick and creamy. Fold in the mascarpone and the grappa, then beat again until smooth.

Put the egg whites in a bowl, whisk until stiff, then fold into the mascarpone mixture.

Make a layer of ladyfingers in a glass dish, dipping each one in the rhubarb juice as you do so. Cover the ladyfingers with half of the rhubarb, then half the mascarpone mixture. Make another layer of ladyfingers and cover with the remaining rhubarb and mascarpone. Cover and refrigerate overnight.

When ready to serve, sprinkle with confectioners' sugar and a little aniseed and decorate with a few whole star anise pods.

Variation Use stewed plums or blueberries instead of rhubarb.

drinks

Think of summer and think of long, cooling, colorful drinks enjoyed in the sun. Start the day with a Strawberry and Yogurt Wake-up Call or a Florida Refresher, go into the afternoon with a Sparkling Iced Mint Tea, then wind down after a long hot day on a Summer Breeze. This chapter is full of traditional and original drinks for every occasion, from old-fashioned homemade cordials, like Lemon Sherbet, to sophisticated cocktails, such as a Bloody Venetian.

florida refresher

Citrus fruits are full of vitamin C, as well as being thirst quenching and invigorating. Bars all over Italy have always been geared up to serve freshly squeezed citrus fruit juices, known as *spremute*. No packaged fruit juice, however good, can compare with freshly squeezed fruit juice. This particular combination of juices and kiwi fruit is sensational.

freshly squeezed juice of 2 grapefruit
freshly squeezed juice of 4 oranges
freshly squeezed juice of 2 limes or lemons

to serve
ice cubes
1 kiwi fruit, peeled and sliced
sparkling or still mineral water (optional)
granulated sugar

serves 4

Put the fruit juices in a jug, mix well, cover and chill until required. Serve poured over ice cubes in tall glasses and topped with a slice of kiwi. Serve with mineral water and sugar for people to add according to taste.

Variation For a weekend brunch treat, add a measure of white rum, gin, or vodka.

al fresco fruit smoothie

Fresh fruit smoothies can be made with any combination of fruit and, needless to say, berryfruits like black currants and raspberries add a lovely color. Try experimenting with different herbs, such as rosemary, thyme, or lavender flowers. You could also try pouring a smoothie over ice cream for a cooling afternoon reviver or a simple dessert, or add lemonade for an old-fashioned ice cream soda.

4 cups strawberries
4 cups raspberries
4 cups melon flesh
4 ice cubes

to serve
4 sprigs of mint or sweet cicely
granulated sugar

serves 4

Put the fruit and the ice cubes in a blender and reduce to a purée. Pour into tall glasses and top with sprigs of mint. Serve with sugar for people to add according to taste.

Variation Try other fruits in season, such as combinations of peach, raspberry and apple; or pear, banana, and kiwi fruit.

strawberry and yogurt wake-up call

There are many types of yogurt, ranging from low-fat yogurt to deliciously rich Greek yogurt, which, sweetened with honey, is breakfast heaven. My favorite has always been plain full-fat yogurt, as its mild, sweet, creamy taste is so good on its own. This energizing recipe can be adapted to suit your tastes as blending yogurt will reduce it to a liquid in any case. If you want to keep it thick, blend the fruit and stir it into the yogurt.

1½ cups strawberries, plus 4 small strawberries, to serve
1 large banana, about 5 oz., peeled
freshly squeezed juice of ½ lemon
2 cups plain full-fat or Greek yogurt

to serve
ice cubes
mint sprigs
granulated sugar (optional)
granola (optional)

serves 4

Put the strawberries, banana, lemon juice, and yogurt in a blender and reduce to a purée. Pour into tumblers, add ice cubes and top with mint sprigs. Cut up into the middle of the four remaining strawberries and "hang" one on each glass. Serve with sugar and granola, if liked, for people to stir in according to taste.

Variation For a weekend brunch treat, add 4 teaspoons of Cointreau.

lemon sherbet

Old cookbooks are full of soft drink recipes, but the advent of manufactured cordials and fizzy drinks has put pay to all that. The high sugar and chemical content of most manufactured soft drinks means that they have little flavor and are not thirst quenching at all. In contrast, this simple recipe for old-fashioned lemonade tastes gorgeous and is totally revitalizing.

thinly pared zest and freshly squeezed juice of
4 unwaxed lemons
3 oz. sugar cubes
1 quart boiling water

to serve
1 lemon, sliced
8 ice cubes

makes 1 quart

Wrap half the lemon zest in plastic wrap and reserve for later use. Put the remaining zest and the lemon juice in a large heatproof jug with the sugar cubes. Add the boiling water and stir, then cover and let cool. Strain and refrigerate. Serve in tall glasses with the lemon slices, a few strips of the reserved lemon zest and ice cubes.

Variation Serve in glasses poured over 2 tablespoons of chopped summer fruit.

sparkling iced mint tea

Cold teas are thirst quenching, stimulating and delicious. Although I use regular tea bags, you could try Earl Grey or other specialist, fruit, or herbal teas. The addition of effervescent liquids turns an afternoon classic into a non-alcoholic party drink, making a welcome change from the usual orange juice and lemonade.

2 tea bags or 2 teaspoons leaf tea
2 cups boiling water
½ cup sugar
freshly squeezed juice of 3–4 limes
2 cups soda water, tonic water or lemonade
4–6 sprigs of mint, plus extra to serve

to serve
1 lime, sliced
8 ice cubes

makes 1 quart

Put the tea bags in a warmed teapot or heatproof jug with a lid and add the boiling water and the sugar. Stir and let stand for 10 minutes. Strain into a heatproof jug and let cool. Add the lime juice, cover and chill until required.

Transfer to a large glass jug and add the soda water and mint sprigs. Serve in tall glasses with a slice of lime hooked over the rim with ice cubes and a sprig of mint in each glass.

Variations Use lemon juice instead of lime juice, or add a jigger of rum to make an evening drink.

melon and ginger refresher

Fresh ginger is often associated with warming winter drinks, but it's also a tasty summer drink ingredient. It is particularly good in non-alcoholic fruit punches, giving them a tangy kick. To crush ice, place the ice cubes in the middle of a clean kitchen towel. Enclose the ice in the towel, grasp it tightly and whack it against the work surface until the ice is crushed.

¾ cup grated fresh ginger
thinly pared zest and freshly squeezed juice of
2 unwaxed lemons
2 cups light brown sugar

to serve
1 small melon, peeled, deseeded, and diced
crushed ice
sparkling mineral water or soda water

makes 1 quart

Put the ginger and lemon zest in a saucepan, add 500 ml of water and bring to the boil, then reduce the heat and simmer for 30 minutes. Add the sugar and stir well until dissolved, then add the lemon juice and strain into a heatproof jug. Let cool, then transfer to screw-top bottles, seal and store in the refrigerator or freezer.

Pour a little of the cordial into a tall glass, add 2 tablespoons of diced melon, fill the glass with crushed ice and top with mineral water. Stir well and serve.

Variation Add a jigger of rum.

trafalgar claret cup

This claret cup packs the kind of punch you cannot ignore and should be sipped not slurped. I would not usually recommend drinking punch with food, but this one retains the roundness of a good glass of red wine and it is not overly sweet, even when made with lemonade. Given its strength, a full Nelson was suggested as a suitable name, but since this year is the bicentenary of the battle, I thought Trafalgar a more fitting name.

¼ cup granulated sugar
1 tablespoon boiling water
1 cup brandy
freshly squeezed juice of 1 lemon
leaves from 6 sprigs of mint, plus extra to serve
4 long strips of cucumber peel
1 bottle (750 ml) red Bordeaux wine
24 ice cubes
3 cups chilled soda water or lemonade

to serve
12 small bunches of red grapes, about 3 grapes in each bunch

serves 12

Put the sugar and water in a heatproof bowl and leave until the sugar has dissolved and the mixture has cooled.

Put the sugar solution into a punch bowl or a large jug, add the brandy, lemon juice, mint leaves, cucumber peel, and wine, cover and let stand for 1–2 hours. When ready to serve, add the ice, stir well and taste. Add soda water to taste. Serve in wine glasses poured over the grapes, topped with mint sprigs.

Variation Add the juice of 1 orange and serve with slices of orange and lemon instead of grapes.

summer breeze

Marinating the strawberries and raspberries in the rum makes for a deliciously fruity drink with a scent of strawberry. The raspberries bleed into the liquid, giving it a pretty shade of pink. Eat the strawberries in your glass halfway down and the flavor changes. This may all sound very light and summery but, mark my words, it's serious stuff.

4 large strawberries, quartered
16 raspberries
3 tablespoons granulated sugar
1 cup white rum
16 ice cubes
1 bottle (750 ml) chilled dry white wine
a dash of chilled lemonade (optional)

serves 8

Put the strawberries and raspberries in a punch bowl or jug, add the sugar and rum and stir well. Cover and let stand for at least 1 hour.

When ready to serve, add 8 of the ice cubes, the wine and lemonade, if using. Put an ice cube and a couple of the raspberries and strawberry pieces in each glass, then pour the fruit cup on top.

1010
1020
CHANGE
FAIR
PLASTIMO
HORN
DIMMER
PIMM'S

john's jug o' pimms

Pimm's is the epitome of English outdoor events in the summer. It comes ready-mixed in a bottle and all you need to do is add lemonade and lots of ice. There are, however, certain essential additions, over and above the fruit, namely cucumber and mint. In days gone by, the fruit was served strung onto toothpicks with the Pimm's poured over it as suggested in the recipe.

8 slices of red apple, such as gala
8 strawberries or cocktail cherries, sliced
8 slices of lemon or orange
8 slices of cucumber
8 sprigs of mint
3 cups chilled lemonade
1 cup Pimm's No 1
ice cubes, to serve

4 toothpicks

serves 4

Put half of the apple, strawberries, lemon and cucumber in a large jug, then add 4 mint sprigs. Add the Pimm's No 1, cover and let stand for 1 hour.

Thread the remaining slices of fruit and cucumber onto toothpicks. When ready to serve, add the lemonade and stir well. Add a mint sprig and ice cubes to each of 4 goblets or tumblers. Fill with Pimm's No 1 and top with the fruit sticks.

bloody venetian

There are so many cocktails that it is almost impossible to create a new one. This is a marriage of two classics, champagne and mimosa cocktails. My own twist is the use of Prosecco wine and blood red orange juice. Prosecco is a sparkling wine made in the Veneto and sold by the glass in bars and restaurants all over Venice; hence the name Bloody Venetian.

2 tablespoons granulated sugar
freshly squeezed juice of 1 lemon
¼ cup Cointreau
¼ cup brandy
3 cups chilled blood orange juice
1 bottle (750 ml) chilled prosecco or sparkling wine
ice cubes, to serve

serves 12

Firstly, prepare the glasses. Put the sugar on a plate and spread it out evenly. Wet the rim of a champagne cup or a cocktail glass with lemon juice and dip it into the sugar, twisting the glass as you do so to get a good covering. Repeat with the other glasses.

When ready to serve, pour the Cointreau, brandy and orange juice into a cocktail shaker and shake well. Alternatively, pour the ingredients into a punch bowl and stir well.

Place a few ice cubes in each of 12 glasses, then pour or ladle the cocktail carefully into the glasses, taking care not to wet the sugar crust. Divide the prosecco between the glasses and serve immediately.

virginia mint julep

This recipe comes from an old American cookbook, *The Williamsburg Art of Cookery or Accomplished Gentlewoman's Companion* of 1742. This is the advice printed with it: "Two Things will inevitably ruin any Julep, the first of which is too much Sugar, and the second is too little Whiskey". Heeding the warning, I have reduced the original quantity of sugar from 6 to 4 tablespoons. The original recipe called for whiskey made from corn, if you can source it, but your favorite whiskey will do.

5 sprigs of mint
4 tablespoons granulated sugar
crushed ice (page 135)
whiskey distilled from corn, such as Kentucky Straight Corn Whiskey

serves 4

Divide the leaves from 1 sprig of mint between 4 tall glasses. Add 1 tablespoon of the sugar to each glass and crush together well using a swizzle stick. Add 1 tablespoon of water to each glass to dissolve. Fill the glasses with crushed ice and add as much whiskey as the ice will take. Stir well until the glasses are frosted on the outside, taking care not to wet the outside of the glass. Decorate each glass with the remaining mint sprigs and serve.

bellini

The Bellini was invented in Harry's Bar in Venice and has become popular throughout the Veneto region of Italy. I first came across Bellinis on a hot August night at the romantic Villa Cipriani Hotel in Asolo in the Veneto hills. No Bellini ever tasted better, but then Italian barmen do have a special way with cocktails.

3 white peaches, peeled pitted
1 bottle (750 ml) well-chilled Prosecco

Put the peaches in a food processor and blend to a purée. Transfer to a jug, cover and chill in the refrigerator overnight or until quite cold.

Divide the peach purée between 6 champagne flutes. Add the Prosecco carefully, then stir and serve immediately.

serves 6

index

conversion charts

Weights and measures have been rounded up or down slightly to make measuring easier.

Volume equivalents:

American	*Metric*	*Imperial*
1 teaspoon	5 ml	
1 tablespoon	15 ml	
¼ cup	60 ml	2 fl.oz.
⅓ cup	75 ml	2½ fl.oz.
½ cup	125 ml	4 fl.oz.
⅔ cup	150 ml	5 fl.oz. (¼ pint)
¾ cup	175 ml	6 fl.oz.
1 cup	250 ml	8 fl.oz.

Weight equivalents:

Imperial	*Metric*
1 oz.	25 g
2 oz.	50 g
3 oz.	75 g
4 oz.	125 g
5 oz.	150 g
6 oz.	175 g
7 oz.	200 g
8 oz. (½ lb.)	250 g
9 oz.	275 g
10 oz.	300 g
11 oz.	325 g
12 oz.	375 g
13 oz.	400 g
14 oz.	425 g
15 oz.	475 g
16 oz. (1 lb.)	500 g
2 lb.	1 kg

Measurements:

Inches	*Cm*
¼ inch	5 mm
½ inch	1 cm
¾ inch	1.5 cm
1 inch	2.5 cm
2 inches	5 cm
3 inches	7 cm
4 inches	10 cm
5 inches	12 cm
6 inches	15 cm
7 inches	18 cm
8 inches	20 cm
9 inches	23 cm
10 inches	25 cm
11 inches	28 cm
12 inches	30 cm

Oven temperatures:

110°C	(225°F)	Gas ¼
120°C	(250°F)	Gas ½
140°C	(275°F)	Gas 1
150°C	(300°F)	Gas 2
160°C	(325°F)	Gas 3
180°C	(350°F)	Gas 4
190°C	(375°F)	Gas 5
200°C	(400°F)	Gas 6
220°C	(425°F)	Gas 7